The ReFirement® Workbook

James V. Gambone, Ph.D.
Erica Whittlinger, MBA
Debby Magnuson
Personnel Decisions International (PDI)

The ReFirement® Workbook

By James V. Gambone, Ph.D.; Erica Whittlinger, MBA; Debby Magnuson; Personnel Decisions International (PDI)

The ReFirement Group® helps individuals and organizations discover the best in themselves through a wholistic and values-based approach to life. The firm offers customized workshops and training programs, consulting services, motivational presentations, and coaching services. Visit www.refirement.com for more information.

Design: Wendy J. Johnson, Elder Eye Design—a design house dedicated to principles of visual legibility and clarity—to create graphics that benefit the eyes of all ages.

Editor: Kristie Nelson-Neuhaus

Copyright ©2004 by Personnel Decisions International Corporation and ReFirement Incorporated. All Rights Reserved. No part of this publication may be altered, translated, reproduced, stored in a retrieval system, or transmitted in any form or by any means, electronic, mechanical, photocopying, recording, or otherwise, without the prior written permission of Personnel Decisions International Corporation and ReFirement Incorporated.

 Personnel Decisions International
2000 Plaza VII Tower
45 South Seventh Street
Minneapolis, Minnesota 55402-1608 USA
612-339-0927

 ReFirement Incorporated
PO Box 142
Crystal Bay Minnesota 55323
866-254-1485
www.refirement.com

Published by Personnel Decisions International.

Printed in the United States of America

Printing Number
10   9   8   7   6   5   4   3   2   1

ISBN 0-938529-27-7

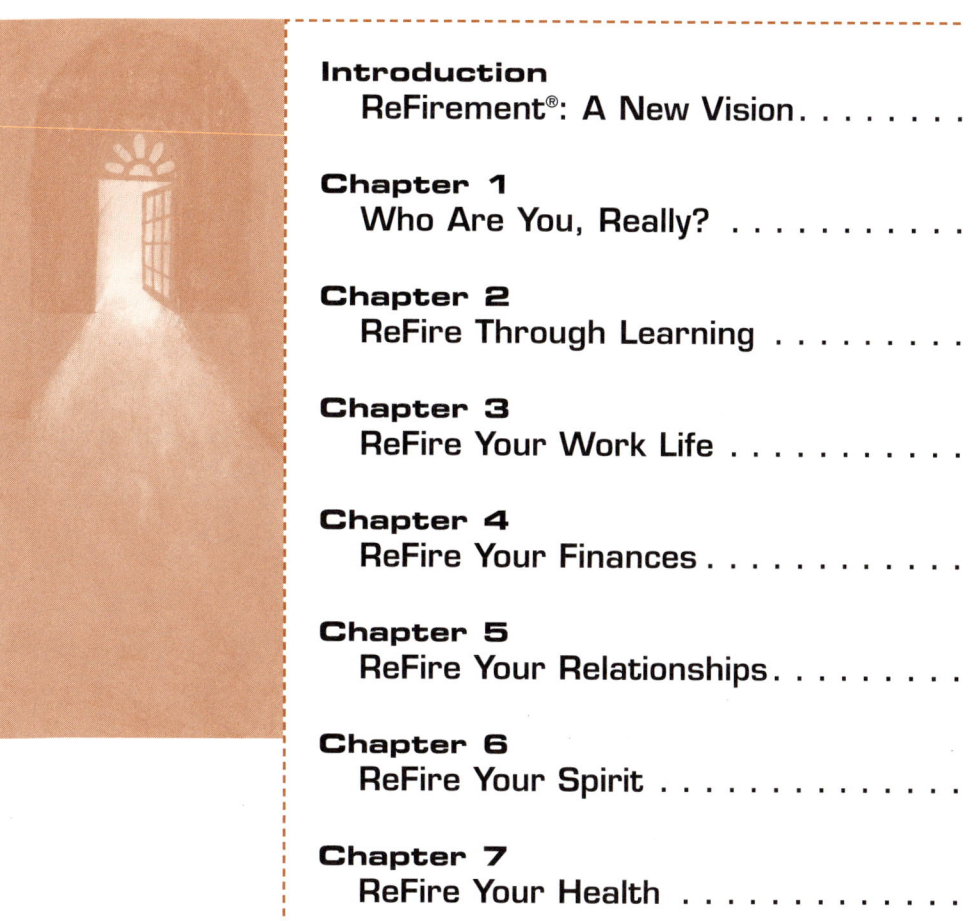

Introduction
ReFirement®: A New Vision 1

Chapter 1
Who Are You, Really? 9

Chapter 2
ReFire Through Learning 17

Chapter 3
ReFire Your Work Life 25

Chapter 4
ReFire Your Finances 37

Chapter 5
ReFire Your Relationships 49

Chapter 6
ReFire Your Spirit 57

Chapter 7
ReFire Your Health 67

Chapter 8
Create Your Own ReFirement Plan 77

Conclusion
You're On Your Way! 91

Appendix
What Do You Expect? 93
About the Authors 96
About Personnel Decisions International . . 97
PDI Offices 98
Development Products from PDI 99

The privilege of a lifetime is being who you are.

— Joseph Campbell

ReFirement®: A New Vision

What comes to mind when you think about planning for the future? Most people focus on two main areas: getting their children through college and saving enough for a comfortable retirement. Pre-retirement planning usually means meeting with a financial planner or attending an employer-sponsored seminar to discuss pensions, Social Security benefits, health insurance, Medicare, and finances. We believe these approaches miss the most important question of all: *What do you want to do with the rest of your life?* With average life expectancies lengthening and medical technology ensuring that most of us will live longer, healthier lives, attention needs to shift to *being* and *doing*.

Fewer and fewer Baby Boomers think of retirement in the traditional sense. They are members of the best-educated, most affluent, and most well-traveled generation in history. They don't plan to bake cookies and putter in the garden when they retire. Many don't want to retire at all. They're asking very different questions: What do I really *want* to do in the next phase of my life? What are my passions and how can I build on them to determine my future? Are there opportunities with my current employer to continue working but for fewer hours or in a different capacity? How can I transform my work skills into meaningful volunteer work? Is it too late to start a new career? What about a starting a small business? And the most haunting question: How can I make sure I reach the end of my life knowing that I lived the most meaningful, fulfilling life possible?

What is ReFirement®?

ReFirement is about being and doing: *Who do you want to be and what do you want to do during the rest of your life?* It starts with your core values, getting back in touch with what's really important to you. It's about your passions, the activities you love to do. It's about setting new goals for this next, exciting phase of your life. And it's about your legacy, what you want to leave behind.

ReFirement's new and optimistic vision for facing the challenges of midlife and beyond will help you create *a plan for the rest of your life's journey of discovery.* The ReFirement process energizes you to make the changes you want, because it is rooted in your heart, mind, and core values. It is a holistic approach that touches every aspect of your life including your learning techniques, health, finances, work, spirituality, and relationships.

ReFirement lights a fire under your passions. There is no more appropriate symbol for the ReFirement paradigm than fire. The ancient Chinese described fire as a connection to life, health, and spiritual energy. They called fire transforming and regenerative. When cultures throughout the world celebrated the millennium a few years ago, they used fire as their symbol for beginning the new century. The act of passing through fire symbolizes transcending the human condition. It is in this spirit that ReFirement will help you recharge and start a wonderful new period in your life.

Is this Workbook for you?

Anyone will benefit from the thought-provoking exercises and personal reflection involved in creating a ReFirement Plan. However, this workbook is dedicated to the Baby Boom and Adaptor generations—110 million members strong—who are heading toward traditional retirement age with lots of new ideas about retirement! Here are basic definitions of these two generations.

- **Adaptor generation:** Born between 1932 and 1944, this group grew up during several wars and faced issues like the Cold War, possible nuclear destruction, and the stirrings for civil and women's rights. All of these factors taught Adaptors profound and valuable lessons. Adaptors tend to be great mediators. They have learned to adapt to a rapidly changing world.

- **Baby Boom generation:** Born between 1945 and 1963, Boomers are the largest generational cohort, 87 million, or one out of every three Americans. This generation has been called idealistic because it has grown up under an umbrella of almost unending economic prosperity. When they were young, Boomers experienced the very divisive Vietnam War, Watergate, and the assassinations of John Kennedy, Martin Luther King, and Robert Kennedy.

Adaptors are sometimes called the "forgotten generation" or the "squeeze generation," and they have made contributions we often don't think about. We call them Adaptors because they bridge the gap between the World War II and Boomer generations, and because their lifestyles have been all about *adapting* to the huge cultural shifts that started in the 1950s and 60s. Think Elvis, the rise of the suburbs, and feminism. Adaptors were influenced by the Women's Movement, and they initiated the increase of women in the workforce. They were the first to demand control over their own health, rejecting the doctor-as-God model, and they have been open to trying alternative methods such as chiropractic and acupuncture. They also experienced, with the Boomers, the disappearance of the implied lifetime employment contract when huge waves of corporate restructuring started in the 1980s. We call Adaptors ReFirement pioneers, because they have truly been on the leading edge of the cultural and social changes of the last half of the 20th century. Now as they reach their 60s, Adaptors are pioneering a new vision of retirement.

Much has been written about the Baby Boom generation, and most of us are familiar with the basic characteristics of Boomers. Based on size alone (87 million men and women, counting immigrants, born between 1945 and 1963), the Boomer generation earns the tremendous amount of attention they have received ever since they started arriving right after the end of World War II. But there is much more than sheer numbers that makes the Boomers different. They were the first generation in American history raised in a culture of abundance and weaned on a plethora of new media dominated by television. These were America-is-the-greatest-nation-on-earth-and-the-sky-is-the-limit! children. Their lives have been characterized by hard work, idealism, and a you-can-have-it-all mentality.

Baby Boomers have strong values and have been accused of being self-absorbed. Work is an important measure of how Boomers define themselves as individuals. The Boomers have challenged every aspect of American culture as they moved through schools and colleges and into the workforce. Now they are challenging traditional concepts of midlife and retirement. Boomers have shown throughout their lives that they believe in self-improvement, education, and the rights of individuals to live up to their fullest potential. Their retirement years will be no different.

The Boomers have followed the examples of the courageous Adaptors by asking the question, "Why shouldn't my work have meaning?" Boomers and

Introduction – ReFirement: A New Vision

Adaptors will continue to ask hard questions as they age. They are rethinking the entire concept of retirement. Given the size of the Boomer generation, they will completely change how our society thinks about the last third of life. Add the realities of medical advances leading to increased longevity, and it is clear that there is a retirement revolution in the works. Together these two generations comprise 110 million men and women. That's almost 40 percent of the U.S. population! As this group ages, it will exercise its political, economic, and cultural power.

What can you expect from this Workbook?

This workbook is based on Dr. James Gambone's inspiring book, *ReFirement: A Boomer's Guide to Life After 50*. The goal of this workbook is to get you started on your own ReFirement process. As you go through the materials, you will read about people who face issues similar to yours. You will have opportunities to reflect and write about your experiences, dreams, and hopes, and you will be challenged to explore your own goals and values through activities and exercises. The chapters in this workbook represent different areas for ReFiring your life: learning, career, finances, relationships, spirit, and health. You can choose to work on one area only, do each of them one by one, or work on them all at the same time. The need and desire for ReFirement is yours, and the pace can be yours too.

By completing the activities in this workbook, you will be ready to develop a comprehensive ReFirement plan that will not only bring you tremendous personal and financial value, but could also add years to your life by instilling a more positive attitude toward your own aging. You will see more possibilities and set a direction for your life that gives you a great sense of excitement and passion. The specific outcomes will depend on how much time and energy you devote to the exercises and your personal ReFirement plan.

We know you are ready to ReFire your life. Let's get started!

Exercise 1: From Retirement to ReFirement!

In the space below, jot down words, images, and ideas that come to mind as you consider the concepts of "retirement" and "ReFirement." What do these concepts mean to you? What is the difference between them?

Retirement

ReFirement

Introduction – ReFirement: A New Vision

The author and philosopher Joseph Campbell said that you must "follow your bliss." Doing what you feel passionate about is deeply satisfying and motivating.

- **What kinds of things do you love doing? Imagine a perfect day. Where would you be, what would you be doing, and with whom? Go for it—no constraints, just your dreams!**

- **What would you do if you followed your bliss? If money were not an issue, what would you do next?**

- **What is holding you back? Is it real?**

Reflection Journal

How does being part of your generation affect the way you look at your life? How are you similar to your parents and/or your children? How are you different from them? What experiences of your generation have brought you to where you are in your life today? Write your thoughts about these questions.

Introduction – ReFirement: A New Vision

 **Next Steps**

How might you carry the values of your generation into your ReFirement process?

1.

2.

3.

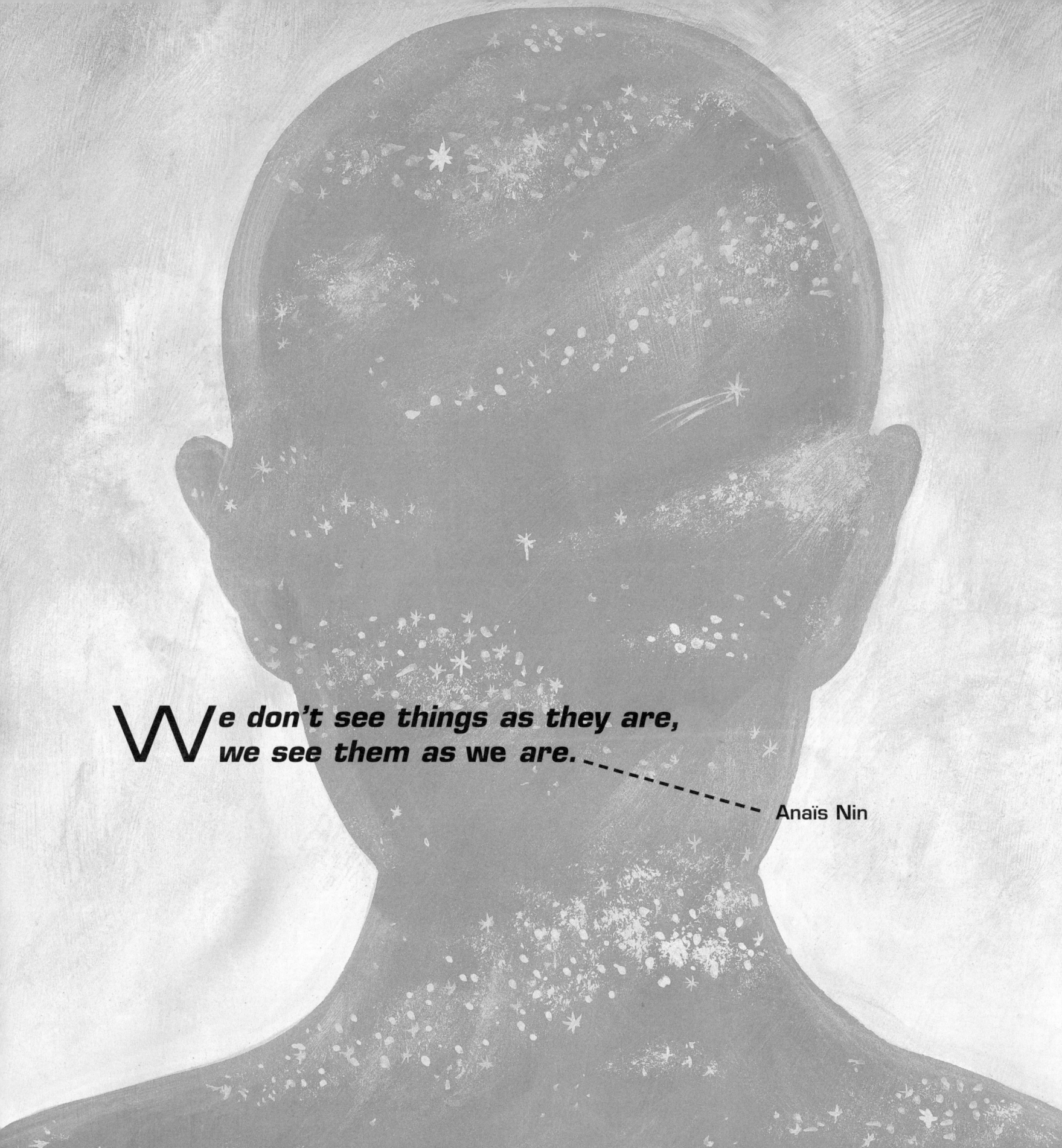

Who Are You, Really?

This chapter is about getting in touch with what is important to you. It is very difficult to chart a path to your future until you better understand your core values and the importance of your hopes and dreams. Exploring core values is a wonderful gift to yourself. In the day-to-day business of our lives, we seldom take time to reflect on the powerful question, "Who am I, really?" This is your chance.

What are your core values?

How many people do you know who have good incomes, important jobs, luxury cars, and beautiful homes, but are not truly happy or satisfied with their lives? The offices of counselors and psychiatrists are filled with people who look as if they have it all. Yet something is missing in their lives. That something may simply be confusion about their core values.

Core values are the deep values you learned at a young age, values such as:
- Honesty
- Belonging
- Respect
- Giving something back through service to others

These basic values tend to get buried by the stuff you accumulate in your life and by things our culture considers important, such as job titles, automobiles, club memberships, and other material possessions. Whether you like it or not, the question of who you truly are often emerges at midlife. You confront events that forever change the way you see yourself. Your children are older and no longer need you in the same way they did. Perhaps someone significant in your life dies, you find out a close friend has cancer, or your career path takes an unexpected turn because of downsizing or a corporate merger. With these life changes, you begin to look much deeper within yourself. When you do, you can find strength in the basic core values with which you grew up.

Honoring your values means living in a way that is congruent with who you really are. Many people experience dissatisfaction and anxiety when they reach midlife and realize that they aren't living their values. If there is dissonance between your authentic self (your values) and how you live (your lifestyle), unhappiness inevitably will result. An important part of ReFiring is living in harmony with who you are by honoring your values.

The following activities will help you identify, clarify, prioritize, and honor your core values by putting them into action.

Exercise 1: Connect with Your Values

In the book *ReFirement: A Boomer's Guide to Life After 50,* we identify previously unreported core values that 75 percent of Baby Boomers have in common. Among them are:

- A Sense of Belonging
- Giving Something Back
- Taking Risks

Most people have missed an important fact about many Boomers: Nearly 75 percent of them grew up poor, working class, or in families that owned a farm or small business. The media and academia have focused on the 25 percent of the generation whose parents had college educations or white-collar professions. The values mentioned above are important even though they are rarely used to describe Boomers or Adaptors. These core values are re-emerging as our population ages. Remembering where you came from and getting back in touch with the values you grew up with can balance the stresses brought on by a culture obsessed with material success. These hidden values, when found, can make a major difference in your life.

Explore these hidden values to discover how they still connect for you. Think about what these concepts meant to you and your family when you were growing up. Is there meaning there for you? How might you get back in touch with these values now?

Complete the following sentences:

When I hear the words **A Sense of Belonging,** I think of _____, I feel _____,

and I want to _____.

When I hear the words **Giving Something Back,** I think of _____, I feel _____,

and I want to _____.

When I hear the words **Taking Risks,** I think of _____, I feel _____,

and I want to _____.

When you have finished the sentences, go back and list an example of when you experienced each of these values. Then, look at what you have written and see what pattern you can discern in your responses. (This can also be an entertaining, thought-provoking exercise to do with others.)

Chapter One – Who Are You, Really?

Exercise 2:
Identify Your Values

Who are you deep down inside? What values describe your most authentic self? Make a list of your most important values. If you find this very difficult, think about people you greatly admire. Think about who those people are and what they do that makes them so admirable. Those traits are probably your values.

What do I value?
Examples: family, integrity, being in nature, faith. Put your own values below.

Exercise 3: Clarify Your Values

Clarifying your values involves a simple test. Pick a value that you consider core from your list above. Then ask these questions:

- Did I choose this value consciously, or did I accept it from somebody else?

- Is it something I regularly act upon?

- Do I practice this value because I want to?

- Do I plan on practicing it for the rest of my life?

- If someone challenged this value, would I be willing to explain it in public?

If you can answer a passionate yes to each one of these questions, that value is true to you.

Chapter One – Who Are You, Really?

Exercise 4:
Prioritize Your Values

From your list in Exercise 2, select the three values that are most important in making you who you are.

1.

2.

3.

Reflection Journal

How do you honor your core values in your life right now?
Which of your values do you wish you put into action more than you do now?

Chapter One – Who Are You, Really?

Next Steps
My commitment to honoring my core values

Reflect on the ideas and concepts you have explored in this chapter's exercises. In the space below, answer the following question: What 5–10 specific actions will I take to honor my core values?

1.

2.

3.

4.

5.

6.

7.

8.

9.

10.

No problem can be solved from the same consciousness that created it.

We must learn to see the world anew.

— Albert Einstein

ReFire Through Learning

As you ReFire your life, it's time to break out of old thought processes that may have kept you from using the best of yourself. What have you always wanted to learn, to try, or to create? Now may be a great time to take a class, go on a trip, read something new, search the Web, or join a discussion group. The opportunities to ReFire through learning are limitless!

ReFired Adventurers
Sue and Pete's story

Sue and Pete always planned to travel more when they reduced their working hours, and they are finally getting the chance to live that dream. Rather than plan trips, they have taken an approach to travel that they find exciting and fulfilling. In the months before they travel to a new location, they use the Internet to research the culture, history, food, and customs of their destination. Then they read books and magazines and seek out local groups from the place they are traveling. They've even taken language and cooking classes to enhance their knowledge. They agree that taking a learning approach has turned their travels into life journeys rather than just trips. As Pete says, "We don't just want to be visitors in this world, we want to be a part of it!" They love their new life, and they look forward to more ReFiring adventures in the years to come.

Like the character Toula in the movie *My Big Fat Greek Wedding*, who changes her whole life when she enrolls in a computer class, stepping back into the role of learner can be the catalyst for ReFirement. Learning something new makes us feel refreshed, renewed, and more energetic. ReFirement through learning can be as simple as doing the crossword puzzle every day or as complex as going back to school for an advanced degree. There is a mounting body of scientific research that shows learning keeps our brains young. Creating new synapses is the key to a youthful mind. We now know that by keeping our brains working and learning, new synapses form whether we're 9 months old or 90 years old. Exciting new research shows that ongoing brain exercise can reduce the risks of Alzheimers. People who remain committed to learning stay engaged in the world and therefore look younger, feel younger, and experience less depression. For many important reasons, it's worthwhile to keep learning!

What kind of learner are you?
Nadia's story

Nadia eagerly signed up for a tai chi class. The instructor taught long sequences of moves, breaking them into steps that the students repeated. Nadia would ask, "What comes next? Where is this going?" Her instructor would reply, "Don't worry about it. Just do this part." Nadia was so frustrated at not having a context for the movements that she quit the class after two sessions.

Rick was an avid skier but even though he wanted to improve his skills, he wouldn't take lessons. "The instructors get so technical, and I really can't concentrate on three things at once. I wish they would just show me what to do, or tell me how to feel."

Joan never met an instruction manual she could use; she was a "pick it up and figure it out" kind of learner. This was true of everything, including her DVD player, microwave, and new Macintosh computer. Her husband Michael couldn't understand Joan's approach at all. Before he touched a new appliance or electronic device, he read the manual through completely, highlighting the key points with multi-colored markers.

People learn in different ways. Learning styles are simply different approaches or ways of learning. There are three universally accepted types of learners:

Visual Learners—learn through seeing. Visual learners usually think in pictures, and they learn best from visual displays such as diagrams, illustrated text books, overhead transparencies, videos, flipcharts, and handouts. You might hear a visual learner say, "I see what you mean."

Auditory Learners—learn through hearing. Auditory learners learn best through lectures, discussions, talking things through, and listening to others. They focus on tone of voice, pitch, and speed. Written information may have little meaning until it is spoken aloud or discussed. You might hear an auditory learner say, "I hear you."

Tactile/Kinesthetic Learners—learn through moving, doing, and touching. Tactile/kinesthetic learners learn best through a hands-on approach, actively exploring the physical world around them. They may find it hard to sit still for long periods and may become distracted by their need for activity and exploration. You might hear a tactile/kinesthetic learner say, "Let's try it out!"

As you review these three learning styles, you may think that you do all of them. That's true; most people use all of these styles sometimes. However, most people find that they have a primary style that they prefer. The following learning styles assessment can help you discover your primary style so you can seek out learning opportunities that work best for you.

Chapter Two – ReFire Through Learning

Exercise 1: Learning Styles Assessment

This chart will help you determine your learning style. Read the word in the left column and then circle the answer in the successive three columns that best describes how you respond to each situation. You may have answers in all three columns, but one column will likely contain the most answers. This will indicate your primary learning style.

When you...	Visual	Auditory	Tactile/Kinesthetic
Spell	Do you try to see the word?	Do you sound out the word or use a phonetic approach?	Do you write the word down to determine if it feels right?
Talk	Do you talk sparingly but dislike listening for too long? Do you favor words such as *see*, *picture*, and *imagine*?	Do you enjoy listening but are impatient to talk? Do you use words such as *hear*, *tune*, and *think*?	Do you gesture and use expressive movements? Do you use words such as *feel*, *touch*, and *hold*?
Concentrate	Do you become distracted by untidiness or movement?	Do you become distracted by sounds or noises?	Do you become distracted by activity around you?
Meet someone again	Do you forget names but remember faces or remember where you met?	Do you forget faces but remember names or remember what you talked about?	Do you remember best what you did together?
Contact people on business	Do you prefer direct, face-to-face, personal meetings? Do you like to communicate in writing through letters or e-mail?	Do you prefer having voice-to-voice contact through the telephone?	Do you need to walk or do an activity while you talk with people? Do you doodle while you listen?
Read	Do you like descriptive scenes, and do you often pause to imagine the actions?	Do you enjoy dialog and conversation, and do you "hear" the characters talk?	Do you prefer action stories or are you not a keen reader?
Do something new at work	Do you like to see demonstrations, diagrams, slides, or posters?	Do you prefer verbal instructions or talking about it with someone else?	Do you prefer to jump right in and try it?
Put something together	Do you look at the directions and the picture?	Do you call a help line to get to talk to a service representative?	Do you ignore the directions and figure it out as you go along?
Need help with a computer application	Do you seek out pictures or diagrams? Do you read the manual?	Do you call the help desk, ask a neighbor, or growl at the computer?	Do you keep trying to do it or try it on another computer?

Adapted from Colin Rose (1987), Accelerated Learning, *and reprinted with permission.*

Just how intelligent are you?

Another aspect of ReFiring through learning is to understand the new theory of multiple intelligences. For a wide variety of reasons, many of us don't have positive memories of traditional learning environments. If you weren't a good student or if you see yourself as nontechnical or not artistic, you may think that taking classes or trying a new learning adventure isn't for you. The good news is that educators have learned a great deal since you were in school about how the human mind learns and what makes a meaningful learning experience.

In the past, measures of intelligence were based on standard I.Q. tests. We now know those are skewed toward certain types of learners—particularly those who excel in taking paper-and-pencil tests—and reflect only certain types of intelligences. In 1983, Howard Gardner, Ph.D., of Harvard University introduced his Theory of Multiple Intelligences (M.I.), and since then our knowledge about how people learn has grown rapidly. Gardner and other researchers and educators now recognize eight human intelligences. Here is a brief overview.

Visual/Spatial Intelligence—the ability to perceive the visual. People who excel in visual/spatial intelligence tend to think in pictures and need to create mental images to retain information. They learn best through looking at maps, charts, pictures, videos, and movies. Their career/hobby interests may include navigator, sculptor, visual artist, inventor, architect, interior designer, mechanic, and engineer.

Verbal/Linguistic Intelligence—the ability to use words and language. People who excel in verbal/linguistic intelligence have highly developed auditory skills and are generally good speakers. They think in words rather than pictures, and learn best by listening, reading, and speaking. Their career/hobby interests may include writer, speaker, journalist, teacher, lawyer, translator, debater, and poet.

Logical/Mathematical Intelligence—the ability to use reason, logic, and numbers. People who excel in logical/mathematical intelligence think conceptually in logical and numeric patterns. They are good at making connections between pieces of information, and they enjoy doing experiments to determine the validity of their ideas. Their career/hobby interests may include scientist, engineer, computer programmer, researcher, accountant, and mathematician.

Bodily/Kinesthetic Intelligence—the ability to control body movements and handle objects skillfully. People who excel in bodily/kinesthetic intelligence express themselves best through movement, whether that's on the tennis court, the dance floor, or in an operating room. They have a good sense of balance and hand-eye coordination. They remember and process information through hands-on experimentation. Their career/hobby interests may include athlete, dancer, actor, firefighter, and artisan.

Musical/Rhythmic Intelligence—the ability to produce and appreciate music. People who excel in music/rhythmic intelligence think in sounds, rhythms, and patterns. They respond immediately to music, and they can be especially sensitive to environmental sounds. Their career/hobby interests may include musician, disc jockey, singer, and composer.

Interpersonal Intelligence—the ability to relate to and understand others. People who excel in interpersonal intelligence try to see things from other people's point of view in order to understand how they think and feel. They are often intuitive and can sense others' feelings, intentions, and motivations. Generally they try to maintain peace in group settings through both verbal and nonverbal language skills. Their career/hobby interests may include counselor, salesperson, politician, and businessperson.

Intrapersonal Intelligence—the ability to self-reflect and be aware of one's inner state of being. People who excel in intrapersonal intelligence try to understand their inner feelings, dreams, relationships with others, and their own strengths and weaknesses. They are best at taking in information that has personal significance to their values and purposes. Their career/hobby interests may include researcher, theorist, and philosopher.

Naturalist Intelligence—the ability to recognize, appreciate, and understand the flora and fauna of the natural world. People who excel in naturalist intelligence have a special affinity for plants and animals, and they have a keen understanding of the role of nature in the balance of life. They are at their best when they can commune with nature, either through growing natural things or through caring for, taming, and interacting with living creatures. Their career/hobby interests may include farmer, horticulturist, landscaper, gardener, veterinarian, and owner/caretaker of pets.

As you read through these brief descriptions of the eight intelligences, there were probably several to which you responded, "Yes, that's me!" In fact, each of us possesses all the intelligences, and we use them all the time. However, we probably have one or two that are dominant.

Exercise 2: What are your key intelligences?

Review the descriptions of the eight intelligences and circle the ones that you feel describe your signature intelligences. Jot a few notes on how your intelligences have helped you in your life. Note any career/hobby interests that caught your eye.

Reflection Journal

Use this space to write down your thoughts or draw a picture about how you can ReFire through learning. What have you always wished you had studied/learned/tried? What are your negative images about learning, and how legitimate are they at this stage of your life? How might you overcome them? What might new learning do for your life right now? How can you integrate your dominant learning style with acquiring new knowledge or skills?

Chapter Two — ReFire Through Learning

Next Steps
Learning Resources

There are amazing resources available to anyone who is ready to get more involved with lifelong learning.

- Public libraries (and those wonderful resource librarians) are great sources of information for low-cost Community Education classes and other learning opportunities in your area.

- Many colleges, universities, and community colleges have classes available to everyone, whether or not you are enrolled in a degree program. Visit a college in your area and see what's available.

- Elderhostel is a not-for-profit organization dedicated to providing extraordinary learning adventures for people 55 and over. In 2003, more than 200,000 people participated in Elderhostel learning programs. Check it out at www.Elderhostel.org, or call their toll-free phone line for personal assistance, 1-877-426-8056.

- Many metropolitan areas have special learning opportunities for older learners. Some examples are the Elder Learning Institute at the University of Minnesota, Bay Area Classic Learning in the San Francisco area, and the Center for Lifelong Learning at the University of Texas at El Paso. The easiest way to find availability in your area is to go to Yahoo.com or your favorite online search engine and search for "Institutes for Learning in Retirement," or "Elder Learning." You will be amazed at the options in almost every state in the U.S. and around the world! Many of these are part of the Elderhostel Institute Network and can be accessed through the Elderhostel Web site at www.Elderhostel.org.

- Volunteering provides rewarding learning opportunities for people of all ages. Your area's United Way or Volunteer Centers are a great way to connect with volunteer options in your community. Find them at www.national.unitedway.org and www.volunteercenters.org

- Another excellent resource for ideas for volunteering is *Golden Opportunities: A Volunteer Guide for Americans Over 50,* by Andrew Carroll (Peterson's, 1994). This is a remarkably comprehensive book that will inspire you to get involved in a way that works for you.

- There are many faith-based learning opportunities available through local religious institutions and national religious organizations. Contact them through your church, synagogue, or mosque, ask your religious leader for ideas, or search on the Web by your denomination's name.

These are just a few ideas. If you're feeling stuck or uninspired, spend a few minutes on a Web site search engine. It will open your eyes to a world of learning options for people of all ages, incomes, and abilities.

It's never too late to be what you might have been.

— George Elliot

ReFire Your Work Life

Creating a ReFirement plan often focuses on work life. This is completely natural since work is such a vital part of life, and because, like it or not, many people find their sense of self through their careers. For a lot of individuals, if work isn't working nothing seems right. More and more Americans report that they feel stress on the job, which impacts their lives in important ways. A 2000 Gallup poll, "Attitudes in the American Workplace," found that 80 percent of workers feel stress on the job and nearly half say they need help coping with it. Dr. Paul Rosch, President of the American Institute of Stress, says, "We estimate [stress] costs American industry 300 billion dollars a year in terms of diminished productivity, employee turnover, and insurance." It is clear that finding enjoyable, rewarding work, even relatively late in life, is a worthwhile and important goal. There are many ways to ReFire your work: take a new job, volunteer, reduce hours to part time, or change the way you look at your current job so you can stay on and feel satisfied right where you are.

Stuck and Dissatisfied
Paul's story

Paul has been a banker all of his life, rising to the position of chief loan officer at a large national bank. Over the years, Paul's original bank was sold twice and merged once. He adapted to the changes but gradually lost any sense of loyalty he had to the institution. More and more, he finds himself bored with his work and dreading Monday mornings. Two college-bound children, a substantial mortgage, growing pension benefits, and his age make him feel that he can't leave. He feels trapped.

In the book titled *No More Blue Mondays,* author Robin Sheerer offers hundreds of practical suggestions for avoiding burnout in the workplace. Two were relevant for Paul. The first is to find a way to reinterpret your existing job and give it new meaning. For example, if you are in manufacturing or product sales, think about how you might sell ideas instead of objects. Or if you are an experienced plumber, you are a pretty good troubleshooter who can quickly assess a situation and take action. What if you were able to translate these skills to other areas of your life? The point is that you can always find new meaning in your work if you seriously decide to look for it.

A visiting missionary at Paul's church talked about starting a microloan program in Colombia. Seed money provided small loans to villagers who wanted to start small businesses. The pastor showed through real-life stories how small contributions made a big difference in people's lives. Paul's eyes lit up when he heard the missionary say that he needed both financial and technical help.

Paul was ReFired. He decided to use his work background and his company's available resources to develop his microloan expertise.

He went to work the following Monday with a new sense of purpose. He contacted the bank's international division and asked what they knew about microloans. He searched the Internet. He inquired about Spanish classes. Most importantly, he called the missionary and told him he wanted to help. Paul's wife was just as excited about the mission loan program as he was, and they have decided to spend their next vacation in a village in Colombia. For Paul there are no more blue Mondays.

Author Robin Sheerer says that by letting your colleagues know that you are there to help serve them, attitudes can change in your work environment. The whole concept of "servant leadership," or leading through serving, captured Paul's imagination as much as the technical aspects of microloan management. Working in a large institution can sometimes feel isolating and not very meaningful. Serving others where you work provides a source of meaning for everyone in the workplace. All of a sudden it's not about the big corporation anymore, but about individual people. You may feel so inspired that you will look for other outlets to express your new approach to work and life.

Chapter Three — ReFire Your Work Life

Exercise 1: Find your passion

Answer the following questions with your first instincts and without editing your responses.

- Is there a career that you wish you had taken up earlier in your life? If yes, what is it?

- What work would you love to do if money were no object?

- What activities are you naturally good at? (Think of things you've been doing since childhood that you don't even remember learning—they just came easily.)

- What types of books do you gravitate to in the bookstore?

- What kinds of work do you find meaningful?

- When you lose track of time because you are totally absorbed, what are you most likely doing?

Exercise 2: Evaluate your career needs

While no work is likely to give you everything you would like to have, identifying your career needs and the extent to which a given job can fulfill them will enhance your chances of meeting most of those needs. When you know what you're looking for and what you need, you can spot the right opportunities.

These exercises will help you clarify the satisfying and dissatisfying aspects of your work. Feel free to add new items or reword the listed items to make them fit your situation.

Preferred work environment

In the Desirable column, put an X by each item that you want in your ideal job. In the Priority column, prioritize each item that you indicated with an X. Give the one you value the most a 1, the one you value next a 2, and so on until you have numbered each desirable aspect.

Aspects of the ideal job	Desirable	Priority
OVERALL PACKAGE		
Job security		
Job location		
Potential for advancement		
Prestige/title		
High salary/wages		
Benefits		
Incentives/bonuses/commissions		
Other		
Other		
TYPE OF BUSINESS		
Mature/established company		
New start-up		
Project/task-oriented		
People/service-oriented		
Technically oriented		

Aspects of the ideal job	Desirable	Priority
TYPE OF BUSINESS (continued)		
Marketing/sales-oriented		
Research-oriented		
Other		
Other		
WORK ENVIRONMENT		
Size of employer (write in size preference)		
Structured work		
Clearly stated goals		
Unstructured work		
Creative atmosphere		
Competitive/action-oriented		
Fast-paced		
Aesthetically appealing environment		
Clear time expectations, set work week		
Individual expression encouraged		
Open communication		
Casual dress		
Private office space		
Fun incorporated into work activity		
Effect on family/personal life		
Other		
Other		

Aspects of the ideal job	Desirable	Priority
LEADERSHIP/MANAGEMENT STYLE		
Hierarchical structure		
Flat structure/shared authority		
Corporate and personal integrity		
Concern with social responsibility		
Other		
Other		
COWORKERS		
Stimulating, creative coworkers		
Cooperative atmosphere/team effort		
Supportive work environment		
Other		
Other		
JOB DUTIES		
Leadership/management responsibilities		
Decision-making authority		
Influence behavior but no direct authority		
Opportunity to gain new skills/experience		
Opportunity for mastery/achievement		
Physically challenging work		
Intellectually challenging work		
Precise work/requires attention to detail		
Variety of tasks		
Control over work schedule		
Travel		
Other		
Other		

Chapter Three – ReFire Your Work Life

Exercise 3:
How well are these priorities being met?

Of the priorities you have ranked as High, indicate which are being met to a satisfactory degree in your current work.

Now list the highest-ranked priorities that are not being satisfactorily met in your current work role.
Write them below, with a brief note indicating what prevents you from achieving them.

Priority   **Obstacles**

Exercise 4: Action ideas to ReFire your work life

What are your ideas for ReFiring your work life? List actions you can take, along with a timeline for accomplishing them and resources to help you. Think big, and think long term. If you've always wanted to go back to school for that master's degree, include it here. If it's time to update your résumé, write it down here. Include actions that will give you emotional satisfaction too, like improving your relationship with a difficult coworker. The power in this exercise is to determine specific, achievable actions you can take toward the work life you want—one step at a time. After all, that's the only way great things have ever been achieved!

Action	Timing	Resources (who/what can help)
Identify coworkers who can support you in the workplace. Ask them for their support.	By June 1st.	Informal times at work when you can talk to these coworkers.
Call or e-mail for educational catalogues to broaden your skills.	By June 15th.	The internet and local or distance learning institutions.

Chapter Three — ReFire Your Work Life

Exercise 5:
Consider ReFiring other aspects of your life

For reasons of financial security, benefits, proximity to retirement age, or lack of options, many people can't simply leave their jobs and find new ones. If this describes your situation, it doesn't mean you're stuck! The key is coming to peace with the fact that you are staying in your job and then renewing your commitment to being the best you can be in your work. What do you enjoy about what you do? Is there a particular part of your job that you like? Can you turn that into an area of expertise that fuels your energy and renews your enthusiasm?

Another approach to finding peace where you are is to ReFire other aspects of your life. Other chapters of this workbook will give you many ideas for how to do this. For example, ReFire your relationship with coworkers, your spiritual life outside work, your health, and your learning. Work on making your financial situation the best it can be. As you feel better about the rest of your life, you will feel more positive about your work life. The choice is yours: bitterness and resentment about what might have been or joy and appreciation for what is.

Reflection Journal

What can I do to ReFire the way I feel and think about my work, in order to enjoy the time I spend there?

Chapter Three – ReFire Your Work Life

Next Steps:
Your work life ReFirement commitment

Review your thoughts and the written exercises from this chapter. What specific action steps will you take **in the next 30 days** to ReFire your work life? Write your specific commitments here:

1.

2.

3.

4.

5.

6.

7.

8.

If money is your hope for independence you will never have it. The only real security that a man can have in this world is a reserve of knowledge, experience, and ability.

— Henry Ford

ReFire Your Finances

ReFiring your finances is all about finding peace of mind as you begin your ReFired life. Many people defer their dreams because of fears (either real or imagined) that they can't afford to live the life they want. ReFiring finances is all about getting in touch with your real financial situation and creating options to move you in the direction of your dreams.

Ted's story

Ted was miserable. He had been offered an early retirement package and desperately wanted to take it. At age 57, Ted had assumed he would work at least another five years. But after receiving the offer to retire early, he just wanted out. He had only two months to decide and felt that the opportunity wouldn't come by again.

The package was a standard one, giving Ted credit for extra years of service in his pension account. His pension payment would be higher than he had already accrued, but less than if he continued to work until he was 62 or 65. His wife Joan was convinced that they didn't have enough money saved for Ted to retire now. Joan planned to keep working for five more years, but she didn't earn enough to cover their current expenses. They couldn't collect Social Security for years, and converting Ted's retirement account to pension payments wouldn't provide quite enough if they both lived to normal life expectancies.

How many times have you found yourself saying, "I'd love to, but I don't have the time" or "I don't have the money"? When you discover what's really important to you, you can reallocate the precious resources of time and money to meet your goals. Going through the ReFirement process—defining your core values and deciding what you really want to do—helps you eliminate the time excuse.

One of the big themes in ReFirement is **options**. You always have options. Unfortunately, our culture is more oriented toward thinking in terms of limitations. Many of us think of money in terms of lack of it—there never seems to be enough. How much money you have or don't have is a result of dozens of decisions (some big, many small) that you make every day. Those decisions are based on your values and priorities. If the lifestyle you choose includes a big house with a three-car garage chock full of late-model vehicles, boats, and other toys, you may have to work far beyond normal retirement age. If you want to ReFire your life, you can allocate money to do what you really want. Make no mistake, this does involve generating options and making choices.

What is your current financial situation?

Ted and Joan visited a financial advisor, who confirmed that their retirement nest egg was not quite big enough for Ted to retire at that time. Ted felt trapped, and wanted to take the early retirement offer, while Joan was fearful for their financial security. The advisor pointed out that they had options they hadn't explored. If Ted worked part time and their income could cover their current expenses, he could defer his pension. After a few more years of tax-deferred growth, it should be sufficient for both of them to retire.

Ted decided to develop a business plan to become a consultant, but he pointed out that he wouldn't even mind bagging groceries at the local supermarket if it meant he could semi-retire now. Ted was inspired by one of his friends who was also offered an early retirement package. She didn't have quite enough money saved but wanted to join the Peace Corps. She said, "I can rent out my townhouse and defer my pension to let it build up. Even though I won't get paid much in the Peace Corps, my living expenses will be covered and I'll be doing good work."

Where does it all go?

Ted and Joan reviewed their expenses and agreed on a semi-retirement budget. They listed their sources of current and future income, including their future pension benefits and Social Security. They also reviewed their investment portfolio, projected its future value, and agreed on the amount of total savings needed for a comfortable retirement.

One of the most valuable financial exercises you can do is to find out exactly where your money is going. At the end of this chapter is a worksheet to help you do this. Go through your checkbook and credit card bills for at least several months (a year is even better) and find out exactly how you spend your money. Don't forget expenses like insurance payments or property taxes that only occur once or twice a year. Put the expenses into categories small enough to be meaningful. You should be able to account for almost all of your income.

What you'll undoubtedly find is that you're spending a lot more on some categories than you thought. Are you getting your money's worth in happiness from those dollars? We all have black holes in our budgets, categories into which money disappears and is never seen again. Watch out for miscellaneous expenses. Many of us spend a considerable amount of money out-of-pocket for lunches, coffee, magazines, etc. It can add up to thousands of dollars a year. Other common black holes include eating out, going to bookstores, buying CDs, making runs to the hardware store, stocking up on shoes—and raising teenagers!

Plugging those holes is like finding money. Just about every one of us can knock five to ten percent off our spending without even missing it, by cutting back on expenditures that don't bring us much joy. That money can be reallocated to what's really important. Financial advisors frequently suggest taking a bag lunch to work, giving yourself a cash allowance each week to limit impulse spending, and eating out less often. One participant in a ReFirement workshop calculated that her morning stop at the coffee shop was costing her $1,000 per year. She bought an espresso machine and put the savings in an IRA. In fact, one fellow we know could have saved $13,000,000 if he had given up the lattes he bought before work every morning. It seems he fell in love with the cute young barista at the coffee shop, and his wife got a huge divorce settlement...

The Expenses Worksheet is divided into three sections for fixed, variable, and periodic expenses. One key to financial freedom is to minimize fixed expenses, those that must be paid and over which you have no short-term control. This includes mortgage payments, car loans, and other types of installment debt; insurance, utilities, etc. To the extent that you can minimize or eliminate fixed monthly payments for loans, you will have more freedom and less dependence on your income. It is much easier to weather financial storms when the overhead you have to pay each month is lower rather than higher.

Make a financial plan part of your ReFirement plan

Ted and Joan had some heart-to-heart conversations about how they each felt about early retirement. Because it was an unexpected change, they needed to talk about how it would affect their relationship, their financial situation, and their plans. Financial security was one of Joan's most important values. She couldn't live with a change in Ted's employment status unless she felt secure. Ted, on the other hand, wanted freedom from his current job.

Ted and Joan's compromise made them both happy. Ted agreed to earn enough to fill the gap in their pre-retirement budget. They both agreed on a level of retirement savings that would calm Joan's fears of becoming old and poor. And in order to increase her comfort level with their finances, Joan enrolled in noncredit personal finance classes at a local community college to learn more about retirement planning and investments.

Exercise 1: Are you a risk taker?

People vary greatly in terms of the amount of risk they can live with comfortably. Early retirement is only one area in which you may be considering taking a risk.

- What kinds of risks have you taken in the last few years?

- How much and what kinds of risk are you comfortable with?

- What opportunities does that include or exclude (e.g., financial, physical)?

Exercise 2:
What do you mean you want to retire?

People have different definitions of retirement. One person may see retirement as the end of a road, while another person may see it as the beginning of a new journey. One couple was shocked when their financial advisor asked each of them when they planned to retire. They had totally different assumptions.

Often, women have an easier time generating work/life options than men. Because many women spend time out of the labor force to raise children, it's easier for them to imagine moving between full-time and part-time work, moving in and out of the labor force, and taking up leisure time avocations. Men tend to think in terms of hard-charging career or full retirement, period.

1. List differences in how men and women approach traditional retirement. (You might want to interview some of your friends for this one. It's a great way to start a discussion at a party!)

2. Choose two or three of the differences you identified and discuss them with someone of the opposite gender, including your spouse or partner.

Issue:

Whom I want to talk with:

What I learned:

Issue:

Whom I want to talk with:

What I learned:

If your ReFirement plan involves starting a business, changing careers, retiring, or modifying your lifestyle, it's important to confirm your actual numbers to ensure that you can fulfill your dreams and stay solvent at the same time. Taking these steps to get a grip on the reality of your financial situation will put you in a good launch position:

1. Go through bank and credit card statements and find out where your money is really going. ("Now" on the Expense Worksheet below.) You may need to keep track of how much cash is dribbling through your fingers for a few weeks.

2. Look for and plug those black holes. Budget less for the stuff that doesn't bring you that much pleasure. Brown bag it now; vacation in Hawaii later. Forecast what your cash flow will look like with your income and newly trimmed expenses. ("Comfortable" on the worksheet.)

3. If you plan to make a big change, such as launching a new business, go over your expenses again. Cut your expenses to the bone and see how little you could live on and how long you could live on it before you'd give up and go back to a "real job." This is also a great exercise in case you suffer a major financial setback such as a layoff. Giving up eating out, vacations, etc., for a few years may be worth it to get what you really want! ("To the Bone" on the worksheet.)

4. If ReFirement means a big change in your life, assessing risk ahead of time will go a long way in reducing your fear. For example, if you want to start a business, take a class and read some books on writing a business plan. Then write your plan and run it by a few experienced entrepreneurs.

5. Determine the worst that could happen (e.g., your career change fails) and what the worst would cost you. Can you live with it? If so, you're ready to launch. Don't forget to factor in your "insurance" elements: being able to cut expenses to the bone, getting financial help from a spouse who works, having low debt and fixed expenses, and so forth.

Always think in terms of options. Don't just think outside the box; get your ReFirement flames going and burn the box!

Exercises 3 and 4 will require time and actual financial information to complete. These two exercises are well worth the time and effort because it is only through this process that you can have a real picture of your finances. This will give you the peace of mind that comes with making decisions based on facts rather than generalizations or fears.

Exercise 3: Where is your money going?

EXPENSE WORKSHEET

Monthly Fixed Expenses	Now	Comfortable	To the Bone
Mortgage	$	$	$
Home equity loan	$	$	$
Car payment	$	$	$
Car payment	$	$	$
Credit card payment	$	$	$
Credit card payment	$	$	$
Utilities: gas	$	$	$
electricity	$	$	$
phone service	$	$	$
cell phone	$	$	$
water	$	$	$
cable/ DSL service	$	$	$
trash removal	$	$	$
Medical expenses	$	$	$
Other _____	$	$	$
Total Fixed Expenses	$	$	$

Variable Expenses

	Now	Comfortable	To the Bone
Gas/bus/parking	$	$	$
Groceries	$	$	$
Eating out	$	$	$
Lunches at work	$	$	$
Household supplies	$	$	$
Dry cleaning	$	$	$
Personal/hair care	$	$	$

Chapter Four – ReFire Your Finances

Monthly Fixed Expenses	**Now**	**Comfortable**	**To the Bone**
Variable Expenses (continued)			
Gifts	$	$	$
Entertainment	$	$	$
Clothing	$	$	$
Magazines/books/CDs	$	$	$
Internet	$	$	$
Health club	$	$	$
Sports activities	$	$	$
Donations	$	$	$
Child care	$	$	$
Education	$	$	$
Other _____	$	$	$
Total Variable Expenses	$	$	$

Periodic Expenses

	Now	**Comfortable**	**To the Bone**
Insurance: auto	$	$	$
homeowner's	$	$	$
medical	$	$	$
Property taxes	$	$	$
Auto: maintenance	$	$	$
repairs	$	$	$
licensing	$	$	$
Home repair	$	$	$
Unexpected expenses	$	$	$
Vacations	$	$	$
Other _____	$	$	$
Total Periodic Expenses	$	$	$
GRAND TOTAL EXPENSES:	$	$	$

Exercise 4: What are you worth?

Most people focus their attention on income, but the real goal should be to increase wealth. List all of your assets and what they're worth. Don't overestimate the value of the "stuff" you own such as furniture. Think big garage sale! List your debts as well. The difference between the two is your net worth—in other words, how much money you'd have if you sold everything and paid off your debts.

List the current market value of your assets and the balances on your debts.

NET WORTH STATEMENT

ASSETS **Liquid Assets**

Checking account .... $_____

Savings account .... $_____

Money market funds .... $_____

Certificates of deposit .... $_____

Other _____ $_____

Liquid Investments

Bonds/bond funds......................... $_____

Stocks/stock funds .... $_____

Cash value life insurance.................. $_____

Other _____ $_____

Retirement Investments

IRAs .... $_____

401(k)/403(b) .... $_____

Annuities .... $_____

Deferred compensation .... $_____

Real Estate

Personal residence .... $_____

Vacation home .... $_____

Investment real estate .... $_____

Chapter Four – ReFire Your Finances

Personal Assets

Automobile	$_____
Automobile	$_____
Household furnishings.	$_____
Jewelry/antiques/etc.	$_____
Other _____	$_____
Total Assets.	**$**_____

DEBTS **Short-Term Debt**
(Loan Balances)

Credit card	$_____
Credit card	$_____
Credit card	$_____
Credit card	$_____
Auto loan	$_____
Auto loan	$_____
Other _____	$_____

Long-Term Debt

Student loans	$_____
Mortgage: primary residence	$_____
Equity line/second mortgage	$_____
Mortgage: other property	$_____
Other _____	$_____
Total Debt.	**$**_____

NET WORTH = TOTAL ASSETS MINUS TOTAL DEBTS $_____

Reflection Journal

What are your feelings about money? What are some of your values about money? How do these feelings and values impact your thinking about your future? Is money holding you back from a fulfilling future? If so, how do you feel about that and what are you willing to do about it?

Chapter Four – ReFire Your Finances

Next Steps:
Streamline and simplify your finances

Over the years, many of us abandon money in various places. We end up with a handful of IRAs, small bank accounts located where we used to work or live, or a 401(k) with a former employer. Your life and tax return will be much simpler if you streamline those accounts. So close the old bank accounts, consolidate your IRAs, sell small holdings—do what you can to simplify your money life.

If you have mutual funds at several different fund families, consider opening an account at Vanguard, Schwab, Fidelity, or an online discount brokerage firm and transfer your funds into it. Transaction fees vary widely among firms. A discounter will charge a small commission for each trade, while other firms charge nothing to buy or sell many funds. Decide which features are most important to you and shop around.

Do you need a financial adviser?
While it's important to be knowledgeable about your financial situation, many people don't like thinking about finances, don't have time to track their investments, or aren't good at it. If you fall into one of those categories, you should work with a financial professional.

Another alternative is to index your investments; i.e., put your money into index funds that track various broad markets such as the S&P 500® or the total U.S. stock or bond markets.

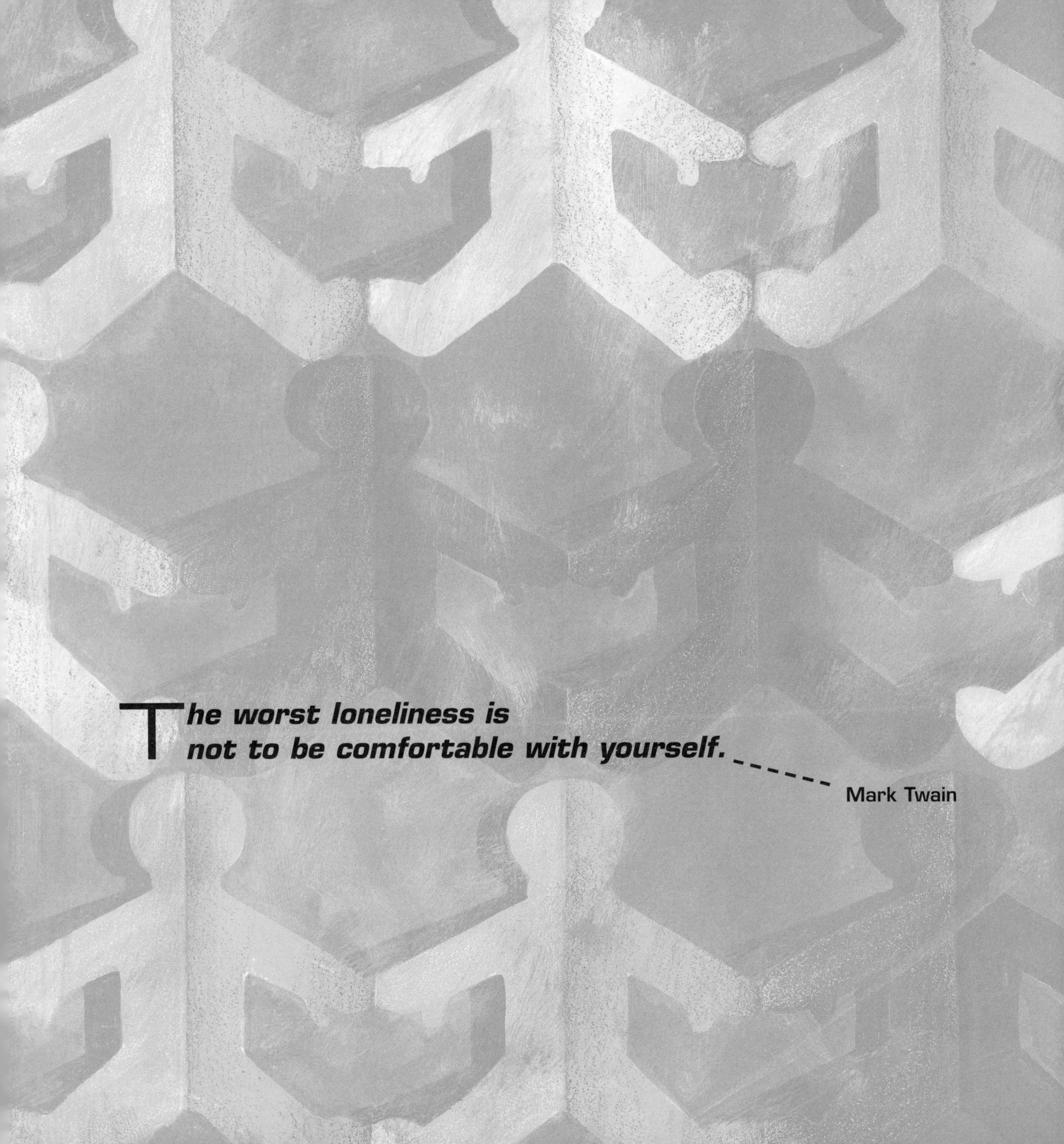

ReFire Your Relationships

ReFirement offers a new opportunity to bring more vitality, mutual love, and depth to all your relationships. The goals of a ReFired relationship are **increased respect, caring,** and **cooperation.** If you have been in relationships without these values (and, of course, we all have), you know how precious (and how worth working toward) they are!

Jeannie and Ed's story

Jeannie and Ed have been married for 28 years. They have two grown children, ages 23 and 26, and one grandchild. Ed owns a successful electrical supply business. For most of their married life, Ed worked 70+ hours a week, and Jeannie handled household, social, and childcare duties. They had a clear division of work and responsibilities that worked well for their family. They experienced some rocky times, especially during the children's teen years, but always felt that they had a happy marriage.

Jeannie loves needlework and crafts. After the kids left home, she found a new vocation as a workshop instructor at a quilt store. With working at the store, preparing for her classes, and doing her own quilting, Jeannie is very busy.

Ed recently sold his business; this has made them financially comfortable. He stayed on as a consultant to the new owner, working two days a week. He never had time to develop hobbies or interests outside work, and he is struggling with how to spend his days off. Like so many men of his generation, Ed found that work was the core of his life. Now he is becoming depressed and difficult to live with. He is increasingly short-tempered with Jeannie, and their interactions often turn into fights, usually about how much time she spends away from home. They are both hurt and bewildered, and each feels unappreciated by the other. It's not a good time in their marriage.

As we reach midlife, our relationships with spouses, children, and other significant people often change. There's a very good reason for this: Our life circumstances are changing, and the way we look at things is changing too. Think about it. The kids are growing up and moving away, our jobs no longer fill the place in our lives they once did, our financial circumstances are different, and our bodies are different. That's a lot of change! It's no wonder that we face challenges in our relationships with those we care about most.

Elliot's story

Elliot was a successful stockbroker with a large brokerage firm in New York City. He often found it difficult to balance the demands of his job with his responsibilities as a husband and a father.

Months ago, he promised his sixteen-year-old son Todd that he would participate with him in a Habitat for Humanity project sponsored by their synagogue. This weekend project was very important to Todd because he was the assistant foreman for this particular house—a role that Todd took very seriously.

However, on Thursday, one of Elliot's top clients unexpectedly decided to visit the firm and stay for the weekend. It was Elliot's responsibility to entertain the client throughout the weekend. Elliot was surprised when his son said, "Dad, do you know how many events of mine you've missed because of business? And how many times we have changed family plans because of business things that "just came up?" When you're gone, what do you want to be remembered for—how many business appointments you kept or how much time you spent with your family?"

As you ReFire your relationships, **you** are the one who is changing; you are the one bringing a fresh perspective. This is where the magic of ReFired relationships lies, because we know we cannot change others. Others may (or may not) respond differently to us as we take a new approach with them. As we ReFire within ourselves, we decide what we want from our relationships and what makes us satisfied and happy, and we create our own change from there.

Chapter Five — ReFire Your Relationships

Exercise 1:
What kind of relationships do you want?

I want a ReFired relationship with:
_____
_____
_____

Complete the following questions for each person you named above:

What do you appreciate most about _____?

What are _____'s best characteristics?

What values do you share with _____?

What do you need most from _____ to support you at this stage of your life? Have you asked him/her for what you need?

What do you think that _____ needs from you to support him/her at this time?

Name five things you could do to increase the respect, caring, and cooperation in your relationship with _____.

1.

2.

3.

4.

5.

Exercise 2: Short-term actions

**Name three specific action steps you can take right now to ReFire your relationship with _____.
By what date will you take each step?**

1.   By ____/____

2.   By ____/____

3.   By ____/____

Who can help? What are some resources (people, books, seminars, etc.) that can offer support in your action plan?

How will you contact those resources? By when?

Chapter Five – ReFire Your Relationships

Exercise 3: Long-term goals

Name some things you've always wanted to do or dreamed about doing to enhance your relationships. (No being practical, no holding back. This is the space for *possibility*!)

1.

2.

3.

4.

Which of these is the most exciting to you?

Why aren't you doing it now?

What would cause you to make that change?

When do you think you will do it?

What could you do within the next three months to begin to make that dream a reality? Six months?

Who could share this dream with you? When will you share it with them?

53

Reflection Journal

As you think about the stories and ideas in this chapter, reflect on your own relationships. What issues are you facing? Write down questions you want to explore, concerns you have, and ideas you want to remember.

Next Steps:
My commitment to ReFired relationships

In the space below, write a brief statement of your commitment to ReFired relationships. Include who is in the relationship, your goals for ReFiring this relationship, and specific actions you are taking to make your goals happen. Make sure that your commitment is not about what anyone else will/should do, only what **you** are doing. You can only control your own behavior, and the power of ReFirement is taking positive action in your own life!

Many men go fishing all their lives without knowing that it is not fish they are after.

Henry David Thoreau

ReFire Your Spirit

ReFiring your spirit is the essence of ReFirement. All of the other elements of a ReFired life (learning, work, finances, relationships, and health) spring from a renewed, energized, and joyful spirit. The inner flame that is your spirit can sometimes be brought low by the pace and distractions of modern life. Why do you think it's called "burnout"? You can kindle your spark through awareness of what spirits you. You can reignite the flame by focusing on the people you love, showing gratitude for what brings you joy, and by allowing yourself to fulfill your deepest wishes.

Eliza's story

At the age of 60, Eliza found herself reflecting on her life. A self-employed professional, she was quite successful in her field. She had two adult children and enjoyed spending time with her grandchildren. After a serious illness, she found herself feeling somewhat empty, as though something were missing in her life. She wondered what her life really meant.

One afternoon, when Eliza was spending time with an old friend, she started talking about a writers' workshop she attends every summer. She said, "You know, I just love to write," and as she talked about writing, her whole being lit up. Her face softened and changed. Her hands flew up to her heart, her eyes closed, and she looked peaceful and happy. She was transformed.

Her friend pointed out that she always "blissed out" at the writers' workshop, yet she never tried writing on her own. Eliza had a standard reply about her clients and the difficulty of getting away from work. Her friend said, "What are you really afraid of?" Eliza said, "I'm afraid I'll end up out on the street with no money and nowhere to go." The two of them started to laugh. Eliza could easily cut back on her hours and workload if she wanted to and still be fine financially, yet she never tried writing.

Her friend said, "You know, you're such a terrific person. Writing makes you so happy. It would be very sad if you died without ever having sung your song."

Each of us has elements in our lives that "spirit" us, that make us feel alive and in the moment. Common activities that spirit us include enjoying nature, humor, being part of a faith community, sports, meditation, being with friends, travel, adventure, pets, hobbies, and music. Unfortunately, the rush of daily life often crowds out activities that nourish us. And sometimes fear gets in the way, especially the fear of trying something new. Often, those fears are unrealistic, but nonetheless prevent us from moving ahead.

As the saying goes, even if you win the rat race, you're still a rat! Our spirits are constantly bombarded by media appeals to the materialistic side of our natures. It is difficult to escape electronic and print advertising on TV, the Internet, radio, in magazines and direct mail, on billboards, and in flyers. While we can turn off the TV and ignore the mail, we're assaulted with video screens in airports, on gas pumps, and in elevator lobbies. There are even ad posters in public restrooms. News media concentrate on bad news, replaying images over and over again, so that many people believe that the world is a much more dangerous place than it is. We are constantly provoked by stimuli that enhance unrealistic fears. The sheer volume of exposure to negative images over time is enough to throw our lives out of balance. We call this being "dulled." Our spirits feel dull, and it becomes difficult to find those parts of us that respond to a higher calling. Here are some signs of our spirits being dulled:

- You don't take time to meet your own needs or take care of yourself.
- You are always saying, "I'm too busy."
- Your consumption of caffeine is getting higher and higher.
- You find it very difficult to pray or meditate.
- You carry your cell phone on the golf course, at dinner, or to other recreational activities.
- You find it very difficult to treat yourself to something special.

Eliza sat down and thought through just how unrealistic her fears were. Her friend was right—finances and clients were not keeping her from writing. This left her asking whether she really did want to write. She decided to challenge herself. She blocked out some time on her calendar to visit her friend's beach house and vowed that she would write for at least four hours a day. What would she learn about herself? What if she couldn't do it? What if she loved it as much as she thought she might? It was time to find out. Eliza scheduled the trip to the beach house, full of anticipation, excitement, and a fear of the unknown that made her feel giddy and very much alive.

Chapter Six – ReFire Your Spirit

Exercise 1:
What spirits you? What dulls you?

Identify your experiences of being spirited and dulled by filling in the following chart.

For example:

I am spirited by…	I am dulled by…
nature	watching television
conversations with friends	repetitious work
reading a novel	reading a user's manual

Your turn:

I am spirited by…	I am dulled by…

After you have completed your columns, choose two or three situations that enliven your spirit. Write a paragraph about each situation, especially how you feel in situations that feed your spirit. If you'd like, talk about them with a family member, close friend, or colleague.

Situation:

Situation:

Situation:

Exercise 2:
Who are the nutritious people in your life?

Many of us realize that there are two kinds of people in the world—"nutritious" people who feed our spirits, and "drainers" who seem to suck the life and vibrancy out of the day. It's very simple to tell which is which. After a conversation with our nutritious people we feel better about ourselves, more positive, and ready to take on the world. After a conversation with the drainers we feel weaker, more pessimistic, and less excited about getting on with life. Nutritious people feed our souls, drainers do just the opposite. What can you do about this very real, day-to-day issue that has a big impact on your life?

Let's face it: As much as you'd like to, you can't always just stop seeing the drainers in your life. Because of family or work relationships, these people may need to be a part of your life. What you can do is be aware of their effect on you and find ways to cope. When we have frequent conflicts with other people, those tensions usually fall into some kind of pattern. Your supervisor unfairly criticizes your latest work effort, and you collapse into a meek, defenseless child. . . again. Your teenager sits in front of the TV rather than doing homework, and you start to nag. . . again.

There's a saying, "If you always do what you've always done, you'll always get what you've always gotten." You can't change other people (Aunt Martha will talk incessantly about the good old days until the day she dies!), but you can change yourself, and how you choose to react. If you change your behavior, it's possible the other person will change his or hers too, because half of the game you two have been playing has stopped.

For example, take time to objectively think about your supervisor's criticisms. How much is legitimate feedback? How much is simply the way he expresses himself, irritating though it may be? How much is small stuff that you can go along with to keep him happy? It has been said, "Forgiveness is letting go." Maybe it's time to let go of irritation and focus on appreciating the good things in your life. When people are irritating or "draining" you, imagine their words simply flying right past you rather than sticking in your craw.

- Make a list of the nutritious people and the drainers in your life. Think about how they affect your spirit and your ability to live your life to the fullest. How can you find more nutritious people? How can you minimize the effects of the drainers?

My Nutritious People

My Drainers

Chapter Six — ReFire Your Spirit

- Ideas for enjoying and encouraging my nutritious people:

- Ideas for coping with my drainers:

Exercise 3:
What's your J.Q.?

We hear a lot about intelligence and I.Q., but what about your "J.Q." —your **Joy Quotient**? Are you actively conscious of being joyful in your day-to-day life? Of having fun? Of living well and laughing often? You can create an environment in which you experience happiness on a regular basis in your life, keep your regrets about the past from inhibiting your ability to change, and look to the future with passion and excitement. What brings you joy? Perhaps it is creating new adventures to challenge your mind and body that ignites your spirit. Or perhaps it's sitting meditatively by the fire, reflecting in gratitude for all the richness in your life. Finding that place of deepest inner joy is different for each of us.

Think of activities you love to do, those that make you feel truly alive, those that make your heart sing. Perhaps it's time for you to take a risk and try something new that could help you feel that inner joy. It might be something you want to try deep down inside, but you've been a bit fearful or hesitant. It could involve shaking up your daily routine, or it could be something wild and crazy. What have you got to lose? Think of all you can gain!

Exercise 4: Your latest triumph

Have you ever done anything in your life that you were told—or told yourself—you weren't capable of doing? Or that you were somewhat fearful or hesitant about? What was it and how did you feel after doing it? Don't worry if it seems like something inconsequential—life is made up of small steps, and they all count towards who you are becoming. Every time you step outside your comfort zone you broaden your possibilities!

What is the most recent activity you have started in your life?

Why did you start it?

How's it going?

Chapter Six – ReFire Your Spirit

Exercise 5:
Push your own envelope

In the movie *The Right Stuff,* one of the original Apollo astronauts was asked what it took to become one of the nation's elite risk takers. He quickly replied, "Being able to push your own envelope."

Write down your ideas for areas where you can push your own envelope during the next year. Don't focus on activities similar to what you already do well. Think of how much more rewarding it will be to try something new!

Tips:
- List at least one thing that will make your friends say, "That just isn't like you!"
- Include at least one physical activity, such as learning in-line skating or yoga.
- Think big, such as a trip abroad.
- Think small, perhaps trying a new cuisine.
- Choose something whimsical like hiring a piano teacher *not* to teach you to play the piano, but just to learn how to play your favorite song.
- Include an adventure you can share with others, such as a hot air balloon ride.
- Keep in mind raising your J.Q.
- Don't rush. Whatever you choose, give it the appropriate amount of time.
- Don't try to become an expert. Do it for the experience and for fun.
- Do it for yourself and not for someone else.

Your turn—go for it!

1.

2.

3.

4.

5.

6.

 **Reflection Journal**

What ideas or thoughts are you most excited about in this chapter? What are your ideas about ReFiring your spirit? Write your reflections here.

Chapter Six — ReFire Your Spirit

Next Steps:
Get started!

Review your list of what dulls and spirits your life, along with your thoughts about your nutritious people and drainers and your wish list. Start replacing the activities that dull you with ones that spirit you. Start building more time into your schedule for the activities and people that spirit you. Choose one activity from your wish list and make a commitment to do it this week. Afterward, reflect in your journal on your thoughts and feelings during that experience. Each week, schedule another activity from your list.

It's not that some people have willpower and some don't. It's that some people are ready to change and others are not.

— Dr. James Gordon

ReFire Your Health

How often do we hear, "If you have your health, you have everything" or "Things might be rough for you right now, but at least you have your health"? But what happens when you *don't* have your health? Almost all of us will face a personal health crisis at some time during our lives. At the same time, facing one's own mortality can stimulate deep thought about what is really important, what you really want to do with the rest of your life, and that your time here on Earth is quite finite. What do you want to be healthy enough to do with the rest of your life? This chapter on ReFiring your health is not about "shoulds." Most of us have more than enough shoulds in our lives! Rather, it is an inspirational approach that helps you explore your health values and then move into action so your body can take you wherever your spirit leads.

Bill and Karen's story

Bill and Karen's lives were stable and productive. They had set down roots in a community they loved. With only their youngest child still at home, Karen returned to teaching and resumed work on her master's degree. Then everything changed in an instant—Karen was diagnosed with stage-three cancer. Her doctors said that she had a 20 percent chance of being alive in five years. Three months later, Bill lost his job.

A life-threatening illness stops people in their tracks. They have to sort through treatment options and alternative and complementary choices. They need help getting to medical appointments, shopping, cooking, running errands, and taking care of children. Many join patient-education and support groups, including virtual communities on the Internet, where they offer support to each other and swap information about the latest clinical trials and research on drugs.

Karen's youngest daughter joined a support group for children whose parents have cancer. Soon Karen volunteered and used her expertise to help the program grow. She added new activities, classroom education, programs for parents, a summer camp program, and reunion parties. This work combined her personal experiences with her teaching skills and love of working with children.

Karen and Bill decided to make the most of whatever time they had left. Traveling was something they enjoyed doing as a family, and they knew it would provide many happy memories in the future. Karen said, "Traveling gives me a short-term goal to look forward to. It's almost like defiance. Cancer is not going to keep me from doing this."

Exercise 1:
The rest of your life

What do you want to be healthy enough to do in the future? Take a few moments to write down some of the things you would like to experience, explore, achieve, have, do, or be during your lifetime. Think about what you would absolutely do if you knew your time was finite.

Ask yourself: "If I could do anything, be anything, or have anything—what would it be?" Don't be constrained by "what is." Complete this section honestly and openly! Use the topics provided here as a starting point, but feel free to add more that are important to you.

1. Family/spouse/significant other relationships

2. Financial status

3. Activities with friends

4. Working hours

5. Community activities

6. Hobbies, leisure activities

7. Cultural activities

8. Travel

9. Other

Chapter Seven – ReFire Your Health

Your ideal healthspan

Many health and longevity experts now use the term "healthspan" rather than "lifespan" to talk about the later years of life. Because of good nutrition, availability of medical care, and advances in technology, people are going to live very long lives. Many Baby Boomers will live into their 90s and beyond. Even now, centenarians are one of the fastest growing demographic groups. Rather than think about how long you want to *live*, think about how long you would like to be *healthy*. For example, if your lifespan is 90 but your healthspan is only 75, you will have 15 years of ill health. Some might call that "health" rather than health!

Exercise 2: What is your ideal healthspan? Who is your healthspan role model?

- What are some of the elements of the quality of life you want for yourself as you reach the later years of your healthspan? What do you want to be healthy enough to do? *Examples: travel, enjoy my grandkids, live independently.*

- Think about people you know in their 80s or 90s whose health and vitality you truly admire. Who are they?

- How did they achieve such excellent health at this stage of their lives?

Bob and Angela's story

Bob and Angela's doctor was pressuring them to do something about their health. Angela was seriously overweight, and Bob's cholesterol and blood pressure were too high. Caught up in their careers and completely sedentary, they hired a personal trainer at a fitness club and started getting up at 5AM for the workout sessions. The trainer put them through a series of exercise machines, insisting that they work on cardiovascular endurance, flexibility, and muscle strength. After two months they quit.

Cancer is an in-your-face illness. Treatments—surgery, radiation, and chemotherapy—are usually harsh and visible to all. But cardiovascular disease, which kills almost twice as many people as cancer, is silent and invisible, accumulating over decades. We hear it over and over again: The best defense against heart disease, stroke, some types of cancer, and other illnesses such as diabetes is a healthy lifestyle that includes cardiovascular exercise, a low-fat diet, maintaining normal weight, not smoking, reducing stress, etc.

We have many options to improve our health. Good health comes from all the seemingly small choices we make every day, such as parking farther from the mall entrance in order to walk a few more steps, ordering a skim latte instead of regular, etc. The road to good health doesn't have to be all or nothing. Every small choice you make to improve your health is one step in the right direction. Put many steps together, and you're on your way to a marathon!

Exercise is the single most important lifestyle change we can make to improve our health, but for many of us it's the hardest. The benefits are many; exercisers even get fewer colds than couch potatoes! Exercise slows the anatomical decline in the brain that starts at age 30, and it improves problem-solving abilities in older people.

A critical component of good health is to get your heart rate elevated and keep it there for 30 minutes a day, five or more days a week. This is a difficult goal for most people, especially those not used to exercise. Forget the fitness books and ignore the torture machines at health clubs. If you're making the transition from couch potato, keep it simple: Find something you like to do and do it every day. For many people, that activity is walking. It requires no fancy equipment, no pre-dawn drive to the club, no lessons and drills. Make the time to take a half-hour walk every day. Over the next two months, gradually nudge your speed up to get your heart going. (Check with your doctor before starting any exercise program.)

Chapter Seven – ReFire Your Health

Exercise 3:
Preventive health practices

To ReFire your health today, what areas do you want to improve?

___ cholesterol	___ weight control	___ sex drive
___ diet	___ dental health	___ blood pressure
___ flexibility	___ strength	___ heart health
___ stress	___ stamina	___ sleep quality and quantity
___ smoking	___ exercise	___ other: _____
___ diabetes/ blood sugar control	___ seat belt use	_____

Exercise 4:
Connect with your health values

Look back to the list of your values you created in Chapter One of this workbook. Which of those values inspires you to make healthier choices? What's the connection for you between good health and living your values? Write down your ideas here.

Value
Example:
Enjoy my family

Connection to my health
I want to have plenty of energy to play with my grandkids

Exercise 5: Get started

What specific actions could you take starting today to incorporate more movement and healthier habits into your life so you can enjoy the good health you want?

Examples:
- Use the stairs instead of an escalator.
- Cut back on butter, sugar, fatty and fried foods.
- When you're outside, notice how good it is to be in the sunshine and fresh air.
- Get white foods off your plate and replace them with red, orange, green, blue, purple, and yellow foods.
- Ride your bike or walk to a neighborhood store instead of driving.
- Pull some weeds in your garden.
- Substitute low- and no-fat dairy products for mayonnaise in your diet.
- Take a walk during your lunch break or after dinner.
- Park at the far side of the parking lot.
- Substitute whole-grain bread for white.

What will you do?
Write your actions toward a healthier lifestyle here:

Chapter Seven – ReFire Your Health

Exercise 6:
Get your heart pumping

Once you get into the exercise habit, you'll feel better in lots of ways. Build movement into your day so it becomes a pleasure instead of a pain. Here are some ideas:

- Really out of shape? Start with 15 minutes of exercise per day and add one minute each day.
- Like to read? Do it while pedaling a stationary bike.
- Record a favorite TV program or rent tapes to watch while walking on a treadmill.
- Try an exercise tape featuring oldies, funk, hip-hop, or Latin music, or one featuring dance steps.
- Set up a regular time to walk with a friend.
- Take a weekly Pilates or yoga class with a friend. It will soon be a social as well as a health activity.
- Purchase an inexpensive pedometer and keep track of your daily steps. A good goal is 10,000 steps per day.

In addition to cardiovascular health through regular aerobic exercise (such as walking or jogging), muscle strength and flexibility are also critical to good health. Make certain you engage in 15–30 minutes of strength training two to three times per week. This could include hand weights, gardening, Pilates, heavy housework, etc. Also, participate in activities such as stretching or yoga to increase flexibility in your joints.

What commitments are you ready to make so that exercise becomes a regular part of your life?

- What exercise options work best for you?

- How often will you do them?

Reflection Journal

Use this space to reflect upon your relationship with your body. What do you appreciate about your body? What do you love the most about it? What would you like to change about it? How does your body serve you well, and how might it serve you better? How could you benefit from enjoying and appreciating your body more?

Chapter Seven – ReFire Your Health

Next Steps:
What works for you?

- What will help you to ReFire your health? Participating in a support group, exercising regularly with a friend, working with a medical professional, watching/listening to video and audio tapes, or reading books and magazines? Make a list of resources that will help you stay committed.

- Enlist the help and support of your family and friends. Bike or walk together. Ban or severely limit junk food. Restock the pantry with wholesome food.

- Once you're hooked on basic get-up-and-move cardiovascular activity, expand your horizons by trying yoga or stretching for flexibility, or simple weightlifting for muscle and bone strength. There are lots of options—classes, books, tapes. Try something new and have fun!

- Health websites to visit:
  - American Cancer Society . . . . cancer.org
  - American Diabetes Association . . . . diabetes.org
  - American Heart Association . . . . american heart.org
  - Mayo Clinic . . . . mayoclinic.com
  - WebMD . . . . webmd.com

Experience is not what happens to you.
It's what you do with what happens to you.

— Aldous Huxley

Create Your Own ReFirement Plan

Chapter 8

Now that you understand ReFirement concepts and have explored them by doing exercises, it's time to create your own ReFirement plan. This chapter is your opportunity to:

- Gather and review information from the activities you did earlier in this workbook.
- Develop your personal portfolio of assets and liabilities.
- Set your ReFirement goals.
- Create a ReFirement plan.

Most worthy projects take concentrated thought and planning. ReFirement is no different. If you truly want to live your life with more energy and intention, you need to take stock of where you are, determine where you want to go, and map out how you're going to get there.

Your big picture of ReFirement

Take a step back to look at the big picture one more time. Based on everything you've learned in this process so far:

- **What do you really, really want?**

- **What will it mean to you to live a ReFired life?**

A good way to begin is to write a Personal Life Mission Statement. Almost every business and not-for-profit realizes at some point they need a mission or vision statement. This statement includes the ideals they want to accomplish over the long haul. The best statements are short and to the point. Your life mission statement will not only give you a clearer direction, but it will enable you to say "no" to something clearly outside of your vision. Don't worry about making the mission statement perfect. You can always refine it. And don't forget to think BIG—this is the rest of your life you're planning here!

Your personal portfolio: What do you bring to your ReFirement process?

Each of us brings a unique set of assets and liabilities to any goal we set or to any change we want to make in our lives. In Chapter One of this workbook, you explored your values and clarified what you think is most important. Use what you learned about your values to help you create your personal portfolio for your ReFirement Plan.

Perspectives on assets and liabilities

Sometimes people feel that their assets column is too meager and their liabilities column is too full. That's when it's helpful to ask someone you trust for his or her opinion. We are usually much too hard on ourselves, so it helps to get another opinion.

During a ReFirement workshop, a woman was having difficulty filling in her assets column. Finally, she reluctantly said that she was a doll maker. The workshop facilitator asked her to list all the abilities she needed to make a doll. She began to list a number of skills and traits: reading a pattern, drawing, sewing, knitting, measuring, patience, and an eye for color and design. After she listed these skills, she felt energized to explore some more.

At another ReFirement workshop, the facilitator watched as a participant encouraged another to talk about *her* assets. But when it was the listener's turn to talk about her assets, she said she couldn't think of any. The facilitator pointed out that, "I've been observing you for about 10 minutes, and during that time you demonstrated that you are a warm, caring, supportive person and a great listener. I bet you have a few other wonderful assets to add to that list." Often, our character traits that we take for granted as being "nothing special" are our best assets!

People tend to view liabilities as something negative and unchangeable. However, liabilities can open your eyes. They can make you more creative and empathetic as you learn how to work with them or in spite of them.

Think of how you could use your assets to counteract or balance some of your liabilities. Say, for example, that you want to start a business. You don't have strong financial skills, but you are very creative, highly persuasive, and have a large network of personal and professional contacts. You probably already know people who could help you, and can convince them that helping you is a good investment of their time.

Chapter Eight – Create Your Own ReFirement Plan

Exercise 1: Mine your assets

List your assets in the space provided below. What are your strengths? What talents and character traits have helped you throughout your life? What about you will make this next ReFired stage of your life successful? These are your personal assets, and we encourage you to mine your assets as you create your plan. Most of us take our strengths and talents for granted, or we don't think we should toot our own horn. It's time to start blowing! Examples of assets include:

- Talents
- Skills
- Personal characteristics
- Experiences
- Important relationships
- Professional and personal networks
- Tangible assets (finances, possessions)

My personal assets

As you create the rich, rewarding life you've always wanted, you will need every bit of talent, wisdom, and strength you have accumulated throughout the years. So dig deep and write down everything that's wonderful about you!

Exercise 2: Acknowledge your liabilities

A liability is something that might hold you back or put you at a disadvantage. What could keep you from doing what you want to do? Keep in mind that your best strengths can become weaknesses in certain situations. For example, being a solid, stable person is a wonderful asset, but it becomes a liability if it means you can't change. Liabilities include:

- Negative life experiences
- Unproductive habits
- Gaps in education or training
- Physical or psychological weaknesses

My liabilities

Write down your thoughts about potential liabilities that could get in the way of achieving your dreams for the next phase of your life.

Chapter Eight — Create Your Own ReFirement Plan

Exercise 3: Review your ReFirement exercises

To start creating your ReFirement plan, look back through this workbook and review each of the ReFirement areas: learning, work life, finances, relationships, spirituality, and health. What did you learn about your core values? What commitments did you make? What ideas excited you the most?

Use the space below to recap and consolidate your learnings from the chapters.
Note: You do not need to have a plan for every area to ReFire your life. If you are satisfied with any of the areas, good for you! Your work there is done. Perhaps you don't want to take on too much at once, so you choose to only work with one area at a time. That's fine too. **This is your process, and you can ReFire at a pace and time that works for you.**

Learning
My ideas about ReFiring through learning:

What I want to accomplish in this area:

Career
My ideas about ReFiring my work life:

What I want to accomplish in this area:

Exercise 3:
Review your ReFirement exercises (continued)

Finances

My ideas about ReFiring my finances:

What I want to accomplish in this area:

Relationships

My ideas about ReFiring my relationships:

What I want to accomplish in this area:

Chapter Eight – Create Your Own ReFirement Plan

Spirit

My ideas about ReFiring my spirituality:

What I want to accomplish in this area:

Health

My ideas about ReFiring my health:

What I want to accomplish in this area:

Create your ReFirement Plan[1]

Now that you have a clearer idea of your assets, liabilities, and a big picture of your ReFired life, it's time to create your ReFirement plan. This is the time for you to think about exactly what you want to accomplish, each step you will take, and whom you will involve. Be very specific, and think about who you want to *be* and what you will *do*.

Thoughts about goal setting:
A goal that isn't written down is just a wish.
The best goals (those most likely to be achieved) are meaningful, exciting, measurable, time specific, challenging, and realistic. The key to setting effective goals is to **get beyond ideas and think about what those goals will look and sound like as you live your plan.** The more specific your plan, the easier it will be to measure success. For example, a ReFired relationship goal to *enjoy my grandkids more* is too vague. What are you going to **do** to enjoy your grandkids more, and when will you do it? *Schedule an outing with my grandkids every other week and plan it with them* is very specific, both in time and actions. You will know if you're achieving it, and you will know fairly quickly if it's a worthwhile goal.

Another example of a too-vague goal is *find more peace and contentment*. It's a wonderful idea but it's too universal. How will you know what to do to achieve it? Again, the key is to get more specific. Each person fulfills a ReFirement dream in his or her own way; there are no right or wrong answers. For some people, the path to peace and contentment is to volunteer with Habitat for Humanity twice a year (specific action with time attached). For others it might be to take a yoga class starting this spring. Your ReFirement plan can help you move from big picture ideas into specific actions. You may not have all the information you need right now and that's OK. Update this plan as often as you need to.

Let's go through each part of the plan.

1. **Focus on your priorities:** Identify your critical issues and development objectives.

   Set goals that are:
   - Meaningful and exciting to you
   - Measurable: How will you know when you've achieved your goal?
   - Time specific: By when will you do it?
   - Challenging
   - Realistic

   Write a short statement describing what it will look like when you achieve your goal. This will be your definition of success.

2. **Implement something every day:** Stretch your comfort zone daily.

   Even the most audacious goal can be accomplished with daily action. Are you willing to spend at least 20 minutes a day building skills and capabilities that will help you create the life you want?

   - If your goal is large, break it into smaller bites, which you can work on each day. Small, concrete actions will help you head off procrastination and make you feel as if you're moving in the right direction.
   - As you complete small steps, you will begin to see progress. You will build momentum. Before you know it, you will be well on your way to your goal!

3. **Reflect on what happens:** Extract maximum learning from your experiences. As you work toward your goals, take time to review and learn from your experiences. Many people find that scheduling time for reflection once a

---

[1] The structure for the goal-setting aspects of the ReFirement plan is based on Development FIRST learning strategies. For more information, read *Development FIRST: Strategies for Self-Development* by David B. Peterson and Mary Dee Hicks, available from Personnel Decisions International.

Chapter Eight – Create Your Own ReFirement Plan

week is a great way to stay focused and on track. **Schedule reflection/planning time in your calendar to make sure it happens.** Otherwise, busyness will get in the way of this important process. Your reflections might include the following questions:

- What is working?
- What isn't working?
- What do you want to continue doing or do more often?
- What do you want to do differently or do less often?
- What do you want to stop doing?

4. **Seek feedback and support:** Learn from others' ideas and perspectives. Learning doesn't take place in a vacuum. Most likely, several people are involved in your ReFirement activities. Actively involve them in your efforts and encourage them to give you feedback. Consider asking friends or colleagues to be part of a small ReFirement group. You can be one another's "front row cheering section" as you meet to discuss your progress toward your ReFirement goals. The advantage of a ReFirement group is that you create accountability for doing what you said you would do. There's nothing like knowing someone is watching to move you into action, and nothing like support and encouragement to keep you going!

Some people shy away from seeking feedback because they assume it will be a negative experience. Try to reframe how you view feedback. Think of it as a conversation that gives you relevant information so you can stay on course. Sharing your ideas, dreams, and goals with others makes them more real. You are putting your intentions out there, which signals commitment to yourself and others.

5. **Transfer learning to the next level:** Adapt and plan for continued learning. The great part about learning is that when you're done, you know more. You can use your new knowledge to help yourself learn the next thing. In other words, you have learned how to learn.

Think of learning as a cycle. When you finish one goal, celebrate your achievement. Then choose your next goal and keep the momentum going. Apply what you just learned to the next series of activities.

Celebrate!

ReFirement is about creating a new reality that is rewarding and exciting. ReFiring your life is reason to celebrate, so take time to bask in your achievements and reward yourself with whatever motivates you to keep moving forward. Here's a toast to you and everything you are doing to live the ReFired life you want!

Your life: a work in progress

Use the next few pages as an outline for creating your own ReFirement Plan. Once you're finished, please realize that you're not finished. If this process works for you, you will probably continue to tweak your plan for the rest of your life. So take some risks, dare to dream, and challenge yourself. You can always come back and adjust to new situations and new opportunities.

My ReFirement Plan

Name: _____   Date: _____

My goal *(Write about each goal separately.)*

    My ReFirement goal is:

    The first step in achieving this goal is:

    I will know I've succeeded in this goal when:

Action steps

    Every day the actions I will take toward this goal are: *(Be specific!)*

    Within a week I will:

    Within one month I will:

    Within six months I will:

Reflection *(Use these questions during your weekly reflection time.)*

    What's working:

    What isn't working:

Things I will do more often:

Things I will do less often:

Resources

Who can help me:

The resources I need to do what I want to do:

Where I will find my resources:

By when:

Transfer the learning

What have I learned in this process that I can use in fulfilling my other ReFirement goals?

Celebrate

What have I achieved?

What's the best way to celebrate my success?

© Development FIRST: Strategies for Self-Development by David B. Peterson and Mary Dee Hicks; and ©1995 Personnel Decisions International.

Next Steps:
Your legacy

A natural consequence of aging is wondering about one's legacy; what will you leave behind? How will you be remembered? Most people focus on wills and estate plans, documents that determine who will receive the material goods they have accumulated over the years. But there is a way to leave part of yourself as well.

The concept of an ethical will comes from Jewish tradition. Jewish tradition says that in addition to passing possessions from generation to generation, we also leave the next generation our values and beliefs. An ethical will is not a legal document, but it can be read after your death. Each ethical will is unique, but most usually contain these elements:

- A list of important spiritual and personal values
- Hopes for future generations
- Blessings for future generations
- Lessons of one's life
- Statements of forgiveness and requests for the forgiveness of others

As you develop your personal ReFirement plan, you'll clarify your important values. Working on an ethical will can complement and enrich your plan as you think about how and for what you wish to be remembered. Creating an ethical will is a wonderful, powerful gift of yourself for the people you love. It can be the most valuable part of your legacy to your family and friends.

Two excellent books can help you write an ethical will: *Ethical Wills* by Barry Baines, M.D., and *So That Your Values Live On* by Rabbi Jack Riemer. Dr. Baines also has a great Web site: www.ethicalwill.com. You can also read more about ethical wills in chapter 11 of the companion book to this workbook, *ReFirement: A Boomer's Guide to Life After 50* by Dr. James Gambone.

Chapter Eight – Create Your Own ReFirement Plan

A journey of a thousand miles begins with a single step. ------- Chinese proverb

You're On Your Way!

Conclusion

We hope you have enjoyed this brief journey into your future. You started by identifying your core values, the foundation that gives you direction and helps you make choices. Your values strengthen your conviction that you know you're on the right track. You need to feel very comfortable with your values as you age because they give you the strength to face obstacles that get in your way.

You now clearly understand that *you* will create the vision of how you age and how you will live the last third of your life. You don't have to follow a retirement vision portrayed by the media, advertisers, and those who prey on your fears about old age to sell products or services. We believe a ReFirement path offers real choices and specific alternatives—paths that are based on your personal values, spiritual directions, financial means, and health status. It is a holistic vision and there isn't one way or a right way to do it. In the end, it comes down to personal responsibility. That's what ReFirement is all about.

The activities in this workbook will give you insights and "ah-has," and will identify additional personal resources you didn't even know were possible. Trust these newfound assets and use them as you move forward.

Finally, your ReFirement Plan will give you an overall road map for what to do next. Remember that maps change when a new road is built or a disaster happens. Your map will probably change many times over the next 10 to 15 years. The good news is that you will no longer be afraid of change, you will welcome it.

You are now ready to begin. Take your personal mission statement and your ReFirement plan and go out there and ReFire your life. You deserve it!

For more ideas and resources, go to **www.ReFirement.com**.

Also, for more books and tips on how to improve your work-related skills, go to **www.personneldecisions.com**. Personnel Decisions International publishes several books that can help individuals improve their work performance.

For one-on-one help and support in your ReFirement process, we have found that it can be helpful to work with a professional life coach or career/business coach.

Begin at **www.ReFirement.com**. In addition to dozens of ideas and resources, the Web site contains names of personal coaches who have been specially trained to use ReFirement Incorporated materials with their clients. While you're there, send us an e-mail telling us your ReFirement story. We'd love to hear about it!

Continue your search at **Personnel Decisions International (PDI)**. PDI's individual coaching services are considered one of the best programs in the country—they have been shown to produce three times the results of other programs. In addition, PDI is the only organization recognized by the Consortium for Research on Emotional Intelligence in Organizations as a model program of best practices in coaching.

Time is one of your most precious assets, and PDI coaches use it wisely. They partner with you to establish the right working relationship and the right process so you can learn as much as possible, as quickly as possible. PDI coaches consistently receive positive feedback on their understanding of business challenges, their expertise, and their caring, supportive styles. Contact PDI at **www. personneldecisions.com**.

For additional background on coaching, visit the International Coaches Federation at **www.coachfederation.org**. Here you will find information on how to connect with a trained professional life coach in your area.

What Do You Expect?

We invite you to find out more about your generation, its values, and unique perspectives by completing the following exercise.

We all live in communities made up of five distinct generations. Our expectations for our lives are shaped by the values of our culture and our time. Read about these five generations, then test your generational knowledge by selecting answers to the questions that follow.

Civic generation: Born between 1910 and 1931. They experienced the Great Depression and World War II during their teen and young-adult years. These events greatly influenced their values and lifestyles. They moved in mass migration to the suburbs after World War II, and they are the parents of the Baby Boomers.

Adaptor generation: Born between 1932 and 1944. This group grew up during several wars and faced issues like the Cold War, possible nuclear destruction, and the stirrings for civil and women's rights. All of these events taught Adaptors many profound value lessons. They tend to be great mediators and have learned to adapt to a rapidly changing world.

Baby Boom generation: Born between 1945 and 1963. Boomers are the largest generational cohort: 87 million, or one out of every three Americans! This generation has been called idealistic because it has grown up under an umbrella of almost unending economic prosperity. When they were young, Boomers experienced the very divisive Vietnam War, Watergate, and the assassinations of John Kennedy, Martin Luther King, and Robert Kennedy.

The Diversity generation: Born between 1964 and 1981. They are also known as **Gen X**. These young people went to daycare in childhood, experienced the job layoffs of their parents, and periods of economic recession during their young, values-forming years. Some served in the Gulf War or watched it on TV. Almost everyone remembers the death of the astronauts in the Challenger disaster.

Millennial generation: Born between 1982 and 2003. As they form their 21st-century values, these Baby Boomers' babies are experiencing the most incredible advances in world communication technology, nanotechnology, and the rebirth of teamwork as a concept in school and the workplace. The experience of 9/11 and living with worldwide terrorism strongly influences this generation.

The **Digital generation:** Born in 2004 and after.

Test Your Knowledge of Generational Identity

What is true for you? *(The answer key follows.)*

Which word would you use to define your generational identity?
- ❏ Civic virtue
- ❏ Individuality
- ❏ Diversity
- ❏ Duty
- ❏ Teamwork

People should get a reward because...
- ❏ They need it
- ❏ It's their right
- ❏ They created it
- ❏ They deserve it
- ❏ They earned it

Work is...
- ❏ A challenge
- ❏ An opportunity
- ❏ An obligation
- ❏ An exciting adventure
- ❏ A way to get there

Education is...
- ❏ A necessity
- ❏ A dream
- ❏ A system
- ❏ A birthright
- ❏ A way to get there

The future is...
- ❏ A time for security
- ❏ Exciting with limits
- ❏ Something to work for
- ❏ Not as important as now
- ❏ Uncertain, but manageable

Communication is...
- ❏ Cordless phones
- ❏ Push-button phones
- ❏ Instant messaging
- ❏ Cell phones and e-mail
- ❏ Rotary phones and letters

Appendix

Answer Key for "Test Your Knowledge of Generational Identity"

Which word would you use to define your generational identity?
- ✔ Civic virtue — Civic
- ✔ Individuality — Baby Boomers
- ✔ Diversity — Diversity
- ✔ Duty — Adaptor
- ✔ Teamwork — Millennial

People should get a reward because...
- ✔ They need it — Baby Boomers
- ✔ It's their right — Diversity
- ✔ They created it — Millennial
- ✔ They deserve it — Adaptor
- ✔ They earned it — Civic

Work is...
- ✔ A challenge — Diversity
- ✔ An opportunity — Millennial
- ✔ An obligation — Civic
- ✔ An exciting adventure — Baby Boomer
- ✔ A way to get there — Adaptor

Education is...
- ✔ A necessity — Millennial
- ✔ A dream — Civic
- ✔ A system — Adaptor
- ✔ A birthright — Baby Boomer
- ✔ A way to get there — Diversity

The future is...
- ✔ A time for security — Adaptor
- ✔ Exciting with limits — Millennial
- ✔ Something to work for — Civic
- ✔ Not as important as now — Boomer
- ✔ Uncertain, but manageable — Diversity

Communication is...
- ✔ Cordless phones — Baby Boomers
- ✔ Push-button phones — Adaptors
- ✔ Instant messaging — Millennial
- ✔ Cell phones and e-mail — Diversity
- ✔ Rotary phones and letters — Civic

About the Authors

(The ReFirement® Group)

Jim Gambone wrote the book *ReFirement: A Boomer's Guide to Life After 50.* As a cofounder of The ReFirement Group, he enjoys helping people find options and meaning in their lives through motivational speaking, workshops, writing, and media producing. Jim is a model for how to ReFire your life and career. He is a successful educator; film and television writer, producer, and director; and an internationally respected expert on generational and intergenerational relationships. Golf, poker, music, and dogs rank high among his passions.

Erica Whittlinger is a case study in ReFirement. A familiar voice for 19 years on Public Radio's "Sound Money" program, she ran a successful money management firm until heart disease convinced her that she literally had a choice between changing her life or dying at her desk. She ReFired by cofounding The ReFirement Group. Her life mission is to inspire people to joyfully live the lives they want to. She holds an MBA and a BA in economics and international relations. Skiing is among her greatest joys.

Debby Magnuson has been ReFiring her life since leaving a 17-year sales training career with a Fortune 100 company in 2002. She has 20 years experience in creating and presenting sales, leadership, and motivational programs. She is a Co-Active Life Coach and is Program Director of ReFirement Coaching. Debby's mission is to kindle energy and passion in her clients' lives and work. She lives in Minneapolis with her husband and two daughters and is discovering the joys of parenting a teenager.

Appendix

About Personnel Decisions International (PDI)

Personnel Decisions International (PDI) is a global consulting firm specializing in talent management. Founded in 1967, PDI is a recognized leader in applying behavioral sciences to help organizations define successful performance; measure capabilities and potential; and develop the skills and abilities of individuals, teams, and organizations.

PDI works with clients to offer integrated, customizable solutions to management and human resources needs. Clients include nearly half of the FORTUNE 500 and many of the Global 1000 companies, as well as large multinational firms and governmental agencies. In 2003, our clients included all 10 companies on FORTUNE magazine's list of *America's Most Admired* companies, and 8 of the 10 *Best Companies to Work For*.

PDI employs more than 250 organizational and counseling psychologists and consultants with Ph.D. or master's degrees. Each of our 28 international operating offices is staffed with consultants experienced in the culture of their particular region, enabling PDI to be a hands-on, strategic business partner and deliver consistent solutions to global clients as well as localized organizations.

Headquartered in Minneapolis, Minnesota, PDI serves clients worldwide with 28 full-service operating offices throughout the United States, Europe, Asia, and Australia. PDI also has strategic alliances with several established consulting organizations in Europe and Latin America.

PDI services and products are based on extensive research and more than 35 years of experience in working with organizations around the world. PDI specializes in helping its clients:
- Select and retain top talent.
- Assess people's capabilities, readiness, and potential.
- Train and develop current and future leaders.
- Coach individuals to change behavior and improve performance.
- Develop a human capital strategy.
- Plan for succession and promote the right people.
- Improve customer relationships.

For more information, contact Personnel Decisions International, 2000 Plaza VII Tower, 45 South Seventh Street, Minneapolis, MN 55402-1608. Telephone: 800.633.4410 or 612.339.0927. Visit our Web site at www.personneldecisions.com.

PDI Offices

The ReFirement Workbook

North America

CORPORATE HEADQUARTERS
2000 Plaza VII Tower
45 South Seventh Street
Minneapolis, Minnesota 55402-1608
Phone 800 633 4410 Fax 612 904 7120

ATLANTA
Suite 560
1040 Crown Pointe Parkway
Atlanta, Georgia 30338
Phone 770 668 9908 Fax 770 668 9958

BOSTON
Suite 401
Three Copley Place
Boston, Massachusetts 02116
Phone 617 236 6511 Fax 617 236 6569

CHICAGO
Suite 2270
225 West Wacker Drive
Chicago, Illinois 60606
Phone 312 251 4180 Fax 312 251 4454

DALLAS - AUSTIN
Suite 1700 LB 142
600 East Las Colinas Boulevard
Irving, Texas 75039
Phone 972 401 3190 Fax 972 401 3193

DENVER
Building One DTC, Suite 925
5251 DTC Parkway
Greenwood Village, Colorado 80111
Phone 303 740 1020 Fax 303 740 0390

DETROIT
Suite 390
100 West Big Beaver Road
Troy, Michigan 48084
Phone 248 619 9330 Fax 248 619 9016

HOUSTON
Suite 700
1300 Post Oak Boulevard
Houston, Texas 77056
Phone 713 499 7500 Fax 713 499 7557

LOS ANGELES
Suite 750
2029 Century Park East
Los Angeles, California 90067-2928
Phone 310 556 4860 Fax 310 556 4865

MINNEAPOLIS - ST. PAUL
2000 Plaza VII Tower
45 South Seventh Street
Minneapolis, Minnesota 55402-1608
Phone 612 339 0927 Fax 612 904 7120

NEW YORK
52nd Floor
405 Lexington Avenue
New York, New York 10174-5301
Phone 212 972 6633 Fax 212 692 3300

SAN FRANCISCO
Suite 310
999 Baker Way
San Mateo, California 94404
Phone 650 372 1090 Fax 650 372 1099

WASHINGTON, DC
Suite 1000
1300 Wilson Boulevard
Arlington, Virginia 22209
Phone 703 522 3519 Fax 703 524 6325

Europe

BRATISLAVA
WBB Slovensko S.R.O. - a PDI company
Tomásikova 14
SK - 820 09 Bratislava
Slovak Republic
Tel 421 2 4333 9368 Fax 00421 2 4341 3977

BRUSSELS
Gulledelle 96
B-1200 Brussels
Belgium
Tel 32 2 777 70 20 Fax 32 2 777 70 30

BUDAPEST
PDI Hungary Ltd.
Victor Hugo utca 11–15
H-1132 Budapest
Hungary
Tel 36 1 350 87 07 Fax 36 1 266 63 60

GENEVA
Immeuble Jean-Baptiste Say
13 Chemin du Levant
01210 Ferney-Voltaire
France
Tel 33 4 50 40 64 11 Fax 33 4 50 40 64 53

GÖTEBORG
Norra Liden 629
411 18 Göteborg
Sweden
Tel 46 31 701 82 12 Fax 46 31 701 82 89

LONDON
80 Wimpole Street
London W1G 9RE
UK
Tel 44 20 7487 5776 Fax 44 20 7487 5356

PARIS
6, square de l'Opéra-Louis-Jouvet
75009 Paris
France
Tel 33 1 43 12 92 92 Fax 33 1 47 42 13 55

STOCKHOLM
Kungsbroplan 3 A
SE-112 27 Stockholm
Sweden
Tel 46 8 402 00 20 Fax 46 8 411 88 30

STUTTGART
PDI Deutschland GmbH
Neue Strasse 7
D-72070 Tübingen
Germany
Tel 49 70 71 55 98 60 Fax 49 70 71 55 98 88

Asia

HONG KONG
Personnel Decisions International Greater China
Suite 3705-6, 37/F
Tower II, Lippo Center
89 Queensway, Admiralty
Hong Kong
Tel 852 2572 2641 Fax 852 2572 2649

SHANGHAI
Personnel Decisions International Greater China
Room 810, Tomson Financial Building
710 Dong Fang Road, Pudong New Area
Shanghai 200122
China
Tel 86 21 5830 9993 Fax 86 21 5830 0907

SINGAPORE
Personnel Decisions International
#24-08 Orchard Towers
400 Orchard Road
Singapore 238875
Tel 65 6732 2252 Fax 65 6733 2252

TOKYO
Yebisu Garden Place Tower 18F
4-20-3, Ebisu, Shibuya-ku
Tokyo 150-6018
Japan
Phone 813 5798 3400 Fax 813 5798 3410

Australia

MELBOURNE
Coyne Didsbury PDI, Pty Ltd
Level 4
398 Lonsdale Street
Melbourne Victoria 3000
Australia
Phone 61 3 9670 3833 Fax 61 3 9600 4001

SYDNEY
Coyne Didsbury PDI, Pty Ltd
Level 2
32 Martin Place
Sydney New South Wales 2000
Australia
Phone 61 2 9235 1516 Fax 61 2 9235 1526

Appendix

Development Products from PDI

SUCCESSFUL MANAGER'S HANDBOOK

Over 900,000 copies in print, this 700-page reference book provides practical tips, on-the-job activities, and suggestions for improving managerial skills and effectiveness.

ISBN: 0-9725770-1-7 $59.95 U.S.

DEVELOPMENT FIRST: STRATEGIES FOR SELF-DEVELOPMENT

This easy-to-read book walks people through proven, practical steps to development. It helps them assess what they should work on, pick the right approaches and tactics, and learn from their experiences.

ISBN: 0-938529-13-7 $16.95 U.S.

LEADER AS COACH: STRATEGIES FOR COACHING AND DEVELOPING OTHERS

Coaching improves the bottom line because it goes to the heart of what makes people productive. This book discusses five practical coaching strategies that will increase the potential of your people and your organization.

ISBN: 0-938529-14-5 $19.95 U.S.

PRESENTATIONS: HOW TO CALM DOWN, THINK CLEARLY, AND CAPTIVATE YOUR AUDIENCE

Practical suggestions will help you develop and fine-tune your skills, from crafting your message to delivering it effectively.

ISBN: 0-938529-23-4 $19.95 U.S.

SUCCESSFUL EXECUTIVE'S HANDBOOK

Drawing from more than 35 years of research and work with executives around the world, *Successful Executive's Handbook* provides business-relevant strategies for improving on-the-job performance and mentoring others.

ISBN: 0-9725770-0-9 $75.00 U.S.

DEVELOPMENT FIRST WORKBOOK

Companion to the *Development FIRST* book, this workbook will help you create and implement a personal learning plan. The workbook comes with fill-in-the-blank templates and a completed sample.

ISBN: 0-938529-21-8 $13.95 U.S.

LEADER AS COACH WORKBOOK

Companion to the *Leader As Coach* book, this workbook offers targeted advice, exercises, and worksheets that will help you develop your coaching capabilities, whether you are a beginner or a seasoned veteran.

ISBN: 0-938529-22-6 $13.95 U.S.

IMPACT WITHOUT AUTHORITY: HOW TO LEVERAGE INTERNAL RESOURCES TO CREATE CUSTOMER VALUE

Strategic Account Managers (SAMs) consistently report that their number one challenge is influencing internally where they have no authority. *IMPACT Without Authority* provides tools, strategies, and approaches that make a difference.

(No volume discounts available)

ISBN: 0-9728836-9-X $19.95 U.S.

Price Grid for Books Listed Above	
Quantity	% Discount
1–9	0%
10–24	10%
25–49	20%
50–199	25%
200+	30%
Plus Shipping and Handling Charges	

Notes: